Albatross

The True Story of a Woman's Survival at Sea

**DEBORAH SCALING KILEY
AND MEG NOONAN**

REPLICA BOOKS

A DIVISION OF BAKER & TAYLOR
BRIDGEWATER, NJ

FIRST REPLICA BOOKS EDITION, MAY 1999

Published by Replica Books, a division of Baker & Taylor,
1200 Route 22 East, Bridgewater, NJ 08807

Replica Books is a trademark of Baker & Taylor

Biographical Note

This Replica books edition, first published in 1999, is an
unabridged republication of the work first published by
Houghton Mifflin, Boston in 1994
Reprinted by special arrangement with
Houghton Mifflin Company

Baker & Taylor Cataloging-in-Publication Data

Kiley, Deborah Scaling.
Albatross : a true story of a woman's survival at sea /
Deborah Scaling Kiley and Meg Noonan. —1st Replica Books ed.
p. cm.
ISBN 0735101345
Originally published: Boston : Houghton Mifflin, 1994.
1. Trashman (Yacht) 2. Shipwrecks - North Atlantic Ocean.
3. Survival after airplane accidents, shipwrecks, etc.
I. Noonan, Meg. II. Title.
G530.T727 K55 1999
910.4/52—dc 21

Manufactured in the United States of America

Albatross

The True Story of a Woman's Survival at Sea

BOSTON   NEW YORK   1994
HOUGHTON MIFFLIN COMPANY

ACKNOWLEDGMENTS

Without the support of understanding friends, family, and professionals, I could not have written this book. Thanks to the Colorado Springs School and Outward Bound for teaching me to believe in myself and for instilling in me the skills necessary to survive.

Thanks to Jill Kneerim, Nina Ryan, Ike Williams, and Art Horan for believing in *Albatross* from its inception. Thanks to Harry Foster for his patience and guidance and to Meg Lukens Noonan for her skill and sensitivity. Thanks also to Nim Marsh and Jeremy McGeary, who were part of the initial seedling from which this project grew. Thanks to Anamika and Anne Hoye for helping me to deal with the stress and anger brought back by reliving these memories and for teaching me to see the light.

And thanks to my family and friends, who stuck by me during the crazy times, never faltering in their support, love, and understanding. Thanks to Bamama, Dad and Betty, Jan White, Diana "Lady-Di" Kirk, Judy Brodkin, Michele Powers, Jane McDonough, Peter Webster, Auntie Skeet and Uncle Jim Calhoun, and Tisa and Dave Brian. A special thanks to Brad, who doesn't always agree with me but still listens, and to my mother, for making me tough.

A very special thanks to the crew of the Russian freighter *Olenegorsk* and Dr. Leonid Vasiliev for their bravery and seamanship, which led to our safe rescue.

Thanks to my husband, John, and my children, Marka and Quatro, for their unconditional love and for always being there.

Who has known heights and depths shall not again
Know peace — not as the calm heart knows
Low ivied wall, a garden close,
The old enchantment of a rose.
And though he tread the humble ways of men
He shall not speak the common tongue again.

Prologue

February 1984
Kennebunkport, Maine

I don't know why I agreed to go surfing on that freezing Sunday in February. I was a lousy surfer and I had a terrible hangover. But a powerful northeaster had just swirled away from the Maine coast, leaving big tube-shaped waves in its wake. Woody convinced me that it was practically my duty to take advantage of these rare conditions.

"Don't be a wimp," he said playfully on the phone,

but he knew that was all I needed to hear. I had never turned down a dare in my life. Maybe it was courage, maybe it was stupidity — whatever it was, I had been born with an extra dose of it. And over the years it had brought me both unbearable heartache and unimaginable joy.

Woody picked me up in front of my rented white clapboard cottage. He was a student teacher at the yacht design school where I was studying.

"Are you alive?" he asked in a morning-after rasp as I climbed into the cab of his old flatbed truck.

"Just barely."

"Good party."

"Great party," I said, rubbing the throbbing place just above my eyelids.

The heater in Woody's truck was blowing cold air on my knees as we drove down the deserted road toward the beach. It was that bleak season on the Maine seacoast between Christmas and the tourist invasion, and everything — the low sky, the barren trees, the empty beach houses, the few patches of gravel-pocked snow along the road — was a sick, lifeless gray.

"Man, is this place grim or what?" I said and kicked at a full bottle of Jack Daniel's lying by my feet on the sandy metal floor.

"That's for later. Have a beer. There's a six behind the seat."

I opened a can of Budweiser and stared out the window. We were passing the White Barn Inn, one of the few restaurants in the area that stayed open year-round.

Smoke was looping out of its chimney, and a few road-salt-coated cars sat in the parking lot.

The closer we got to the beach, the more I wished I was back at the White Barn sipping a bloody mary, mopping up hollandaise sauce with an English muffin. Instead I was freezing my butt off in this broken-down truck, and my head was killing me, and I was going surfing.

We pulled up in front of the broad, hard-packed beach and parked. The ocean was dark and wild and nastier-looking than I'd ever seen it here before. A half-dozen surfers were straddling their boards out beyond the spot where the steep waves were breaking. Two surfers paddled after the same big swell, but before they got to their feet on their boards, they were catapulted off as if they'd been shot out of a cannon.

"Shit. They're big," I said and drained the beer in one long gulp. I was starting to feel queasy. Deep breaths, I told myself, deep breaths. My hands were tingling. I hated feeling this way. Once I had loved the sea more than anything — even at its most powerful. Now it terrified me.

"All right!" Woody drummed on the steering wheel with his fists. "Guaranteed instant hangover cure."

He got out of the truck and hauled the surfboards from the back. Tucking one of the boards under his arm, he ran to the water, hollering for me to follow. I got out of the truck, picked up the board, looped the leash around my ankle, and made myself walk toward the surf.

By the time I got to the water's edge, Woody had already disappeared behind the waves. I stepped in. Even with a wetsuit on, the cold made me gasp. I lay down on the board and paddled as fast as I could out past the breakers.

I was alone. Woody and the others were a little farther out, hidden behind the huge shoulders of dark water. My teeth were chattering. Straddling the board, I rose and fell with each big swell. I don't want to be here, I said to myself, and then screamed it into the wind. I don't ever want to be in the ocean again!

I looked back and saw a big wave curling toward me, so I lay down and started paddling hard. I felt the wave lift me up, and suddenly I was speeding toward the beach. When the board skidded onto the sand in a bath of white froth, I jumped up and dragged it out of the water. My whole body was shaking.

Maybe I could just sit in the truck until Woody comes in, I thought. I said I'd surf and I did. I did one — that ought to be enough. Woody rode a wave in toward shore, flopped off the board, and motioned to me to come back out. Okay, I'll try one more. Then I'm coming in. I'll just go after an easy one, a nice little cruiser.

I paddled out again, riding up and over the big seas. I straddled the board and took a couple of deep breaths. Suddenly an enormous wave was above me, curling, collapsing, dragging me down into its turbulent wake. The leash jerked backward, pulling me down — or up? — I couldn't tell. I needed air, but I was being held under. Hot needles of panic pierced my body, and all at once the memories were rushing in, and once they started I couldn't stop them.

4

It all came back: the boat and the storm and the wind and the sharks and the cold and the fear, the terrible ice-blue fear. I wanted it to stop, but I was rolling and choking and falling, and I couldn't get up and I couldn't stop any of it.

I managed to fight to the surface, then gagged and vomited into the water. Another wave hit me, and I was sucked down again, tumbling backward until my shoulder scraped bottom. There was another wave and another. I was totally disoriented, out of control, unsure if the sky was above or below. Finally I felt my feet slam onto the sand, and I dragged myself out of the water. Crying and choking, I staggered toward the truck.

The awful things I had tried to bury were everywhere now; in the thundering surf I heard screams, in the rotting kelp I smelled decaying flesh. I got into the truck and slammed the door. Then I put my forehead on my knees and cried.

"What are you doing in here?" Woody asked as he opened the driver's door. "You're missing all the best waves."

"I have to go home," I said. I had been in the truck for twenty minutes and couldn't stop trembling.

"You cold? I was afraid that wetsuit was too big for you."

"I have to go home now." I stared straight ahead.

"What's the matter? Feel sick?"

"I just have to go."

"Well, can you hang on a sec? I was kind of wanting to go back out."

"Could you just please take me home now," I said slowly. Keep breathing, I said to myself. Keep breathing.

"Okay, all right. Let me put on some dry clothes. Don't you want to change? You look frozen —"

"No. I mean it, Woody," I said and started to sob again. I couldn't stop myself. "I have to go home. Just get in the fucking truck and take me home!"

"Okay. I'm coming. Take it easy?"

He got in and started the truck.

"I'm sorry," I said and covered my face with my hands.

Woody drove me home in silence. Everybody at school knew I had been in a bad boating accident. But Woody and I had talked about it only briefly, and though he had tried to be sympathetic, I knew he couldn't begin to understand what I had gone through.

Looking back, I can see that I hadn't begun to understand it either. I thought I was handling it all pretty well. I was tough . . . I could cope. Just like riding a horse, Deb, I told myself. Just climb back on.

I rarely talked about what had happened to me in October 1982. I had tried to toss away the terror like some foul bag of garbage. I thought that if I did normal things like go to class and watch television and go to parties I would *be* normal. But I was wrong.

When Woody pulled up in front of my house, I jumped out of the truck, ran in, locked the door, and fell against it. And then I cried. I cried until it was dark, then got into bed and cried until it was light again.

For the next three weeks I hid behind that locked door, not answering when my friends came looking for me. I didn't go to school. I barely ate. When I did eat, I finished the meal by sticking my finger down my throat and making myself sick. I wanted to get it out — I wanted to get everything out of me.

The only people I talked to were my father in Texas and my mother in New Orleans. My father listened and struggled to find comforting words. My mother tried to be supportive, but I could tell she didn't want to hear any more about my problems. God knows she had enough of her own to deal with. Holding the phone with two hands, I told my parents over and over again, in a voice I hardly recognized as my own, that I was going insane and I had to leave this place.

My father finally said he would send me a plane ticket. I didn't know what I would do once I got to Texas. I just knew I had to go. I had to escape the things that were making me crazy: the constant talk of boats, the smell of low tide, the people who kept telling me how lucky I was to be alive. How could I explain to anyone that I didn't feel lucky? That being alive felt more like a curse than a gift?

✔

I was rescued at sea on October 28, 1982. I was a "survivor" — that's what it said in all the newspaper accounts. But it took me almost ten years to feel like one. In the decade after the accident I was in a perpetual storm, one as real and frightening and unfathomable as the one that sank my boat. The storm began to abate only when I began telling people what had happened. Now, as I sit down to write my story, I can finally say with conviction that the wreck of *Trashman* was the worst thing that ever happened to me. And it saved my life.

1

Early September, 1982
Bar Harbor, Maine

It was only a few days after Labor Day, and already the light over Southwest Harbor had changed. All of the milky vagueness of August was gone, replaced by a sharp-focus world of color and possibility. I stood at the top of the long wooden dock at Hinckley's Boatyard and breathed in deeply. Low tide, a smell that always made me happy.

A few hundred yards offshore a yellow catboat, its

broad sail lit by the morning sun, tacked slowly between the huge moored yachts. I walked to the end of the dock, sat down, and dangled my legs above the water. I'd seen a lot of harbors in the last three years, but this was one of the prettiest, with its low rounded mountains, quiet sapphire water, and tall pine trees bordering the shore. It was beautiful here now, but I knew that in a month the winds would come in from the north and temperatures would drop. It was definitely time to move on.

I'd been in Maine since June. After sailing in a yacht race from France to Louisiana, I had decided to spend some time on dry land. I went to stay with my mother in New Orleans, but as usual we were quickly at each other's throats. Within a week she had made it clear that she wanted me to leave.

I had boarded a northbound bus and ended up in Bar Harbor with less than five dollars in my pocket. After sleeping in a pup tent for a few weeks I found a waitressing job at Bubba's, a popular restaurant. I'd been there all summer. Now I had an apartment, a couple thousand dollars saved up, and a few friends. But I also had a massive case of sailing fever.

What I wanted more than anything was to get back on the water. I had spent most of the last three years on sailboats. I'd knocked around the Caribbean doing charters and some racing, then had sailed to England and talked my way into a job as a cook on a boat entered in the year-long Whitbread Around the World yacht race. Then I'd joined an all-women crew for the transatlantic race back to New Orleans. I had needed a break — but now it was time to sail again. I had started asking around for a local boat that might need crew, and soon the captain of a yacht moored in Southwest Harbor came in to Bubba's to tell me he was hiring crew for a delivery to Fort Lauderdale.

I spotted the gorgeous green Boothbay Challenger on her mooring a few hundred yards from the dock. *Trashman* was painted in gilt across the stern — what an ugly name for a pretty boat. John Lippoth, the captain, climbed down from the deck and got into a Zodiac tied to her side. As he steered the small red inflatable dinghy toward the dock, the tiny motor barely ruffled the calm waters. He waved to me and I waved back.

"Sweet day, huh?" he said, pulling the Zodiac up to the dock and tossing me the painter. He pushed up the brim of his salt-stained blue cap. His narrow eyes had the deep squint lines of a man who had spent much of his life on the water.

"Makes me want to be sailing," I said.

John picked up a canvas briefcase and climbed to the dock. He was so skinny his jeans looked as if they might drop to his ankles with one wrong move. His droopy blond mustache made his thin face look even longer. I figured he was five years older than I was — twenty-nine or maybe thirty.

"I just have to make a quick call," he said. "Mind waiting here a minute? Then we'll go take a look."

John hitched up his paint-splattered jeans and headed up the dock. I could hear the buzz of power sanders coming from one of the big metal-roofed hangars in the boatyard. There was something magical about knowing that back there somewhere a Hinckley sailboat — the Rolls-Royce of yachts — was being built. I didn't care if John took an hour; I was content just to sit there.

After about ten minutes he came back.

"Climb in," he said. "Sit up there."

John started the motor and pulled a Heineken out of a small plastic cooler.

"Want one?" he asked as he flipped off the top. I shook my head. He took a long drink from the bottle, ran his tongue along the bottom edge of his mustache, and gunned the engine. The bow of the Zodiac lifted as we accelerated, and I grabbed the polypropylene line attached to the gunwale. Buzzing across the harbor, I felt the fine salt spray and the sun on my face, and I was instantly happier than I had been in months.

As we came up on *Trashman* I could see she was different from anything I'd sailed on in a long time. A ketch rig with a graceful sweep to her sheer, she was sleek and well balanced. Her hull was a rich piny green, and there was just enough teak trim to make her look elegant but not so much that she would be tough to maintain. She had an unusually large white deckhouse with three big windows on each side.

She did need some cosmetic work. John had told me that he had taken over just a few weeks ago, and it was obvious he hadn't had much time to spruce her up.

I checked out her rigging and saw that she was dressed in all the latest cruising gear — roller-furling jib, mainsail, and mizzen; electric winches. A gleaming white fiberglass Dyer Dhow dinghy was suspended from davits off the stern.

"Not too shabby, huh? It's an Alden design. They only made four of them," John said. "The owner's loaded. He made it all in the dumpster business or something."

"Trash man?"

"You got it."

"Weird name for a boat, though."

"Yeah."

"Does she handle well?"

"Not bad for a cruising boat."

I followed John around the deck. The owner had obviously outfitted the yacht for ease and comfort. This kind of rigging was fine for cruising yachts, but I knew that what you gained in convenience you often sacrificed in performance.

When we went down the companionway to the main salon, I was amazed at how bright it was. It seemed an outrageous luxury to have that kind of light belowdecks. I was used to the dark, dungeonlike cabins of racing boats. There was an L-shaped settee on the port side and two fancy upholstered chairs on the starboard. Yeah, I thought, I could get used to this; I'd had enough of cramped racing boats, wet bunks, and freeze-dried food to last me a lifetime.

"She's fifty-eight feet, but she seems a lot bigger, don't you think?" John went to the stereo and popped in a tape. Steve Winwood's voice came blaring out of the speakers. "Come on, I'll show you the crew quarters and the galley."

I followed him down a short flight of steps to the galley. Dirty dishes and coffee cups were piled high in the small sink. Empty Heineken bottles covered nearly every flat surface, and an open bag of potato chips was lying on the floor.

"Kind of a mess right now," John mumbled and steered me forward. Just across from the galley was another stateroom with two bunks, one above the other. The crew cabin was a triangular space in the bow with bunks on each side, a small head, and lots of storage space for sails and other gear. I could see that no crew had slept here in a long time. Sails, bags, lines, and tools were strewn everywhere.

"I'll show you where I'm camped out." John shut the door to the crew quarters and led me back past the companionway, then down a few stairs next to the instrument panel on the starboard side. A short hall led to the big master stateroom, which had oversized bunks on each side and a spacious head with a shower.

"Pretty nice," I said. Both beds were unmade, and rumpled clothes and empty bottles were everywhere. The air smelled of cigarette smoke.

Back in the salon, John disappeared toward the galley and came back with two Heinekens. "You look thirsty," he said. I took the bottle from him.

"So, here's the deal," he said, lighting a cigarette. "Like I told you at Bubba's . . . I need a combination cook and deckhand — somebody who can help me get the boat cleaned up. In a couple of weeks we'll pick up crew and head to Florida."

I nodded my head.

"First of the year, we head to the islands, get the owners, and do some cruising."

"Sounds good," I said. I didn't tell John that all I really wanted was a ride to Florida. Maybe I'd like being on *Trashman* so much that I would spend the whole winter on her, but for now I wanted to play it by ear.

"So I guess I should ask you some stuff and then you can send your résumé to Morris Newberger — he's the owner — and see what he thinks."

"Okay."

"You said the other night you had done some racing?" John crossed his legs and began picking at a hole on the sole of one of his battered boat shoes.

"Yeah, I did the Caribbean thing — charter boats mostly — a couple of winters ago, and I wound up in Antigua for Race Week in 'eighty-one. Then I sailed to England on a ferrocement ketch. After that I did the Whitbread on *Xargo*."

John took a long drag on his cigarette and said nothing for a moment. I was used to lengthy silences when I told people I had sailed in the Whitbread — the first American woman to complete it. Often they were skeptical, but I had done the whole thing. I'd rounded Cape Horn, been battered by sixty-foot waves in the Southern Ocean, seen whales and albatrosses — and cooked for ten men who treated me as, alternately, their mascot and their slave.

"*Xargo?*"

"The South African boat."

"I thought the Whitbread didn't take girls," John said.

"I kind of talked them into it."

"What did you do for them?"

"I was the cook, but you know how it is on boats — I ended up doing a little bit of everything. I was gone for about a year."

"I know a guy who did that. He said it was hell. He couldn't wait to get off." John stood up and went to get another beer. I showed him I was still working on mine.

"It's not for everybody, for sure," I said, loud enough to be heard in the galley.

"I'd rather be in the islands," John said as he came back into the salon. He took off his cap and ran his hand over his thinning, sun-bleached hair. "Guess you wouldn't have any trouble sailing this thing?"

"I don't think so."

"Let's see, what else . . ." John looked uncomfortable. "Geez, I'm hungry. You want to go grab some lunch? There's a place next to Hinckley's. The Moorings."

I followed John up to the deck. He seemed like a nice guy — kind of awkward, maybe, but pleasant enough. I was relieved that he wasn't looking at me as anything other than a crew member. I'd been around enough boats and sailors to know that sailing together sometimes leads to sleeping together. All I wanted from John was a ride south.

While John went to untie the Zodiac, I stood on the deck and looked out at Cadillac Mountain. Some of the trees near its bald summit had already turned red. I breathed in deeply and smelled the warm spiciness of the sun-baked teak. Nothing in the world could match that smell. I made up my mind right then that if the money was decent and John offered me the job, I would take it.

We took the Zodiac back to the dock, then walked up to the Moorings, a seafood and chowder place with big windows overlooking the harbor. I would have liked to sit at a table that looked out on the water, but John went straight for the bar. The bartender immediately flipped the top off a Heineken and put it on a round cardboard coaster in front of John.

"Gee, come here often?" I said.

He ordered a hamburger, and when I said I'd just have a small salad, dressing on the side, he groaned.

"No wonder you're so skinny," he said.

"Oh, yeah, real skinny," I said.

"You're a twig. C'mon, have a burger or something. I'm buying."

Food had been a problem with me for years. I'd been fighting bulimia ever since I was shipped off to boarding school as a gawky teenager. This summer I had been struggling — not very successfully — to get it under control. I told the waiter the salad would be plenty.

While we ate we talked about sailing and mined each other's pasts for mutual acquaintances. There weren't many. I had sailed mostly offshore or from Europe. John said he had grown up in Maine and had taught sailing in summer. He told about some of the boats he'd worked on. I figured he had to be good to have landed a position as captain of *Trashman*.

When we finished lunch, John said he would call

Newberger that afternoon, and he reminded me to mail my résumé. Newberger lived in Dallas. I was born on a ranch in Throckmorton, Texas, and I figured that once he saw where I was from I'd be a shoo-in.

✓

A week later I found John sitting at the Moorings bar tapping a box of cigarettes on the heel of his left hand.

"Hey," I said. John looked up. His eyes were bloodshot.

"No word yet from Newberger," he said. "But you'll get it, I'm pretty sure."

"Great. I really want to do it."

"Tell you what," he said, pulling a cigarette out of the box. "Think you could still work nights at Bubba's and help me get the boat ready during the day?"

"I could probably work it out."

"There's a bunch of things I haven't gotten around to . . ."

I thanked John and turned to leave.

"Hey, where ya goin'?" he said. "Stick around. Have a beer with me. We should celebrate."

John waved his hand at the bartender.

"A coupla more greenies?"

I sat back down. What the hell, I thought. I didn't have to be at work until four-thirty.

I spent the next three weeks working on *Trashman* by day and at Bubba's by night. It felt good to be doing the physical work of prepping a boat for sea. And *Trashman* responded well to my efforts. John had assigned me all the "domestic" chores — cleaning out the lockers, restocking the galley, getting gear organized — as well as some of the cosmetic deck work. He was handling everything else.

I found out right away that John was not the hardest worker in the world, nor was he the most reliable. On my first morning of work he was a no-show at the dock, and I had to bum a ride out to *Trashman*. When I got on board, I found him passed out in his bunk with all his clothes on, mouth open and snoring. When he finally woke up he spent the next hour groaning and staring into his coffee cup.

More than anything else, John liked his little "celebrations." We celebrated my first day of work by going ashore for a three-hour lunch. And to celebrate the day Newberger officially approved of hiring me, we headed into Bar Harbor and drank our way from one end of town to the other.

The last boats I'd been on had been temperamental, high-maintenance racing machines. Nobody screwed around — at least not until the race was over. There was always a deadline or a start to get to or the next leg of the race to prepare for. I was used to busting ass to get everything bought, made, or repaired. And I was used to working for skippers who were perfectionists.

But with *Trashman* there was no urgency, no sense of needing to be prepared. We'd be at sea for only a couple of days at a time at most. John said we would pick up what we needed when we needed it. It didn't matter to me if he wanted to piss away the days. I assumed that when we finally went to sea he would get serious.

One rainy afternoon at the Moorings, John pulled his neatly typed résumé out of his canvas briefcase and handed it to me. I made some obligatory crew-to-captain remarks about how impressive it all was. And it was true, there were some great boats on the list, but none of his jobs seemed to have lasted long. When I asked him about it, he told me that personality conflicts or scheduling glitches or sudden changes in plans had always cut short his employment.

His last job had been on *Black Knight,* a black-hulled eighty-eight-foot powerboat that I had seen once in Newport. John said he had worked on that boat with his girlfriend, Meg Mooney.

"Why isn't she on *Trashman?*" I asked, knowing both that it was none of my business and that John had enough of a buzz going to tell me.

"Newberger told me not to hire her."

"Why'd he do that?"

"We had some problems on *Black Knight.* Coupla fights. Nothing big. Coupla bigwigs got ticked off."

"Newberger knew about it?"

"He heard somewhere. Said Meg couldn't go. Isn't that bullshit?" John asked as his elbow slipped off the edge of the bar.

I'd seen plenty of shaky relationships explode in the close quarters of a boat. But I'd never heard of it getting so bad that the couple was blacklisted. I pressed John for details, but he didn't seem to want to talk about Meg.

"Don't give a shit anyway," he mumbled, an unlit cigarette dangling from his mouth. He was fumbling with his lighter. I handed him some matches off the bar. "We broke up. Tha's it. She really was a bitch. Who needs tha' shit?"

I had no intention of getting involved in John's love life. I stayed busy doing my projects on *Trashman* and kept things light between us. When he wanted a drinking buddy, I was usually willing. When he wanted to be alone, I kept my distance.

Things were going so well I even managed to have a few decent telephone conversations with my mother. But when she said she was thinking of coming north to visit my half-brother, Lee, a college student in Boston, and me in Bar Harbor, I panicked. My mother was not your usual sort of mother, if there is such a thing. Her life — and, as a result, my life — had been one long, crazy soap opera.

The daughter of a wealthy Texas rancher, she married a local cowboy at seventeen, then gave birth to me and divorced my father before she was twenty years old. Now a recovering alcoholic, my mother was a great beauty who believed in the importance of appearances. She hated the idea that her only daughter was knocking around in boats. I had never been able to please her — not as a small child, not as a smart-mouthed teenager, and certainly not now. I'd always felt she blamed me for every rotten thing that had happened to her, and I knew we would resume the same old battles when I saw her again.

She arrived on a sunny, cool morning, and all went well for the first few hours. John and I took her out in the Zodiac and circled *Trashman* so she could get a look at it. Afterward we all had lunch at the Moorings. My mother was in rare form, and John seemed captivated by her. I knew it was easy to be dazzled by this charming, perfectly coifed woman if she didn't happen to be your mother. But I was a wreck. I found myself shoveling a cheeseburger into my mouth as fast as I could and ordering apple pie with vanilla ice cream — and waiting for the right moment to bolt for the ladies' room and purge myself of it all.

"Why are you wasting your life this way?" my mother asked me later, after we had driven back to her fancy inn in Northeast Harbor. "When are you going to settle down?"

"Don't start, Mother."

"I don't care at all for that John fellow. There's something strange about him. I don't think I approve of you just going off with him —"

"You're such a good judge of character —"

"Pardon me? What did you say?"

"He's all right. You don't even know him."

"Are you doing something different with your hair?" she said, reaching to brush my bangs to one side before I could duck.

By the time Mother left, after three days, I had thrown up half a dozen times.

A week or so later, John came into Bubba's and stood by the waitress station looking impatient. When I was finally free to talk, he said, "Newberger called. He wants us to get going."

"What's the hurry?" I asked, hoisting a trayful of sandwiches onto my shoulder.

"I don't know. He says get going. We gotta go."

"I told my boss I was here for another couple of weeks."

"Tell him there's been a change in plans."

"I'll ask."

"We have to make a stop in Portland to get some documentation papers from the Coast Guard. Then we'll head for Newport. And we'll probably hit Annapolis in time to catch the boat show. That's always a good time."

"I'll ask."

My boss agreed to let me go if I would work one last weekend. John and I made plans to have our last dinner ashore — another celebration. We would take off on Tuesday. John said we'd overnight in Camden, where he hoped we'd be able to pick up some more crew. He hadn't been able to find anyone but me in Bar Harbor.

I packed my few belongings into a duffle and spent the night before we left in the crew quarters. I was so excited I couldn't sleep. As I lay in the narrow bunk and felt *Trashman* bouncing a little in the light chop, I heard the cries of geese passing over. They were heading south — to hot sun and turquoise water. I'm right behind you, guys, I thought, and closed my eyes.

2

"Okay, Deb. When you're ready, cast off," John said. I liked his low-key style, especially in early morning, before the caffeine kicked in. Most of the captains I'd sailed with barked out orders like drill sergeants.

We had been up since before dawn. I had tied the Zodiac off the stern, uncoiled the sheet tails and dropped them on the deck next to the winches, taken in and stowed the fenders, straightened up below, and put a second pot of coffee on. Now, on John's command, I stood on the mooring pennant to get a little slack in it, pushed the marker buoy out, slipped the loop off the bitts, and dropped it over the bow roller. As the line sank, John went to the cockpit, gave the wheel a spin to starboard, shifted forward, and applied some throttle. Then he turned up the volume on "Arc of a Diver." "If you see a chance, take it . . ." he sang along, bobbing his head to the beat between sips of coffee.

I let out line on the Zodiac until John was happy with where it rode in our wake, then went back to the cockpit to prepare to raise the mainsail.

"Don't bother," John said. "There's not much wind. We'll just motor. You want to do something, how 'bout some breakfast?"

I went down to the galley. John was probably right about the wind. It could take us all day to get to Camden under sail. I resigned myself to being on a motorboat for a while. There would be plenty of sailing soon enough.

After breakfast John asked me to steer, and I jumped at the chance to find out how *Trashman* responded to the helm. What I discovered was a little disappointing. She was slow to react and felt heavy. I reminded myself that that wasn't unusual for a sailboat under power. I'd give her a chance to prove herself once we raised her sails.

For the next few hours John studied navigation charts while we threaded our way through the maze of rocky islands along the Maine coast. Early in the afternoon we eased our way into Camden's pretty harbor, secured

Trashman, and headed up the main street to a couple of bars where John thought we could "get a line on crew." Besides, he said as he opened the door at O'Neill's, "we have to celebrate our first day on the water." John asked a few people if they might want to crew, but aside from one babbling drunk, no one seemed interested.

The next day we motored to Portland and spent the night tied up at DeMillo's Marina. John talked me into going out on the town again — "hair of the dog, Deb" — and we spent another long night doing a tour of his favorite watering holes. Early the next morning we took on fuel, then motored a few miles north to Falmouth Foreside, John's home port. His father had kept a boat here for years, and his mother still lived a few miles away. John borrowed a car from her so he could drive into Portland to pick up some documents for *Trashman.* When he returned he said the papers wouldn't be ready for a few days.

I was disappointed. Now that we had started the trip, I wanted to keep going. I couldn't wait to get to Florida. The days were getting shorter, the nights colder. We still hadn't found any extra crew, and with only two of us on the boat we wouldn't be able to sail through the night. Already it looked as if the trip was going to take a lot longer than I had expected.

That night John headed into town to meet someone, and I stayed on the boat, glad to have some time alone. I settled into a chair with a glass of wine, my dog-eared copy of *Shogun* — and my own music, for once, on the stereo. It was peaceful in the lamplit cabin. The boat bobbed easily at her mooring. I could hear the slapping halyards on the few yachts anchored near us. Occasionally a boat would pass and *Trashman* would roll in its wake, then settle down again. I went to bed early and slept so soundly I didn't hear John come aboard.

Sunlight filtered through the small window in my cabin. I could hear John rummaging around in the galley. It wasn't like him to be up before me, especially after he'd been out late. I got up, ran my fingers through my hair, and poked my head out of the cabin, saying, "What are you doing up?"

Then I saw that it wasn't John in the galley. It was a woman.

"Oh," I said.

"Hey, there. You must be Debbie. I'm Meg."

"Meg."

"A friend of John's. Want coffee?" She handed me a cup.

She didn't look at all the way I had pictured her. She had shiny black hair down to her waist, pale skin spattered with freckles, and piercing blue eyes. She was too striking and sophisticated-looking to be called pretty — and she had to be at least five years older than John.

I sat down, and Meg lowered herself into the chair opposite me. She crossed her long legs just so, as if she were posing for a catalog. She pulled a long brown cigarette out of a pack on the table, lit it, and took a deep drag with her fingers held straight. Her nails were perfect. She fixed her eyes on me and smiled a perfect smile.

28

"So. John tells me great things about you," she said. "I think we're going to have fun."

I gave her a dopey grin. Fun. Did she say fun? Did she say we?

John appeared in the doorway. He looked as if he hadn't gotten much sleep. "Oh, good, you met," he said. "Is there coffee, babe?"

Meg sprang from the chair and went down to the galley. I glared at him.

"What is she doing here?" I whispered.

"She wanted to see the boat," John said.

"I thought she wasn't supposed to be on board."

"She was at my mom's last night. I brought her back to see the boat. Take it easy. It's just for the weekend. I thought she'd like to go for a sail."

Meg reappeared, handed John the coffee, and kissed his unshaven cheek.

"This boat sure is beautiful," Meg said. She had one of those cigarette-lowered voices and a soft southern drawl. "Kind of cozy and elegant all in one, don't you think?"

"Mmmmm," I said.

"You're keeping her up real well. That's not easy with John around," she said, looking at him with obvious affection. Our little bad boy John. I gulped my coffee and burned my tongue.

"John said you race?"

"I have," I replied.

"The Whitbread, wasn't it?"

"Uh-huh."

"Well, better you than me, honey. I like boats when

the sun is shining and the water is flat. Right, John? I'll make some breakfast." She stood up and pranced back into the galley.

John was poking at buttons on the navigation instrument panel and making notes on a yellow pad. He glanced up at me, then looked down quickly. When Meg came back, John declared, with more enthusiasm than I had heard from him in a month, that the weather tomorrow was going to be so wonderful we absolutely had to go for a sail. This from the man who had yet to raise one sail since I had come aboard. So now he wants to go sailing, I thought. Well, well . . . John Lippoth was full of surprises.

Meg's arrival clearly called for a celebration. John suggested we all head into town for lunch.

"That sounds great," Meg said. "Doesn't it, Debbie?"

"Mmmmm," I said.

While Meg cleared the coffee cups, I went up on deck. As I walked to the stern I could hear raised voices from the cabin below my feet.

". . . lying son of a bitch," I heard Meg saying.

"What?"

"You told me she was a dog."

"I never said dog . . ."

"She's not ugly, John. As if you haven't noticed. You two been having a nice little cruise? Pretty cozy on your big fancy-ass yacht?"

"You know it's not like that," John said.

"Don't tell me what it's like. I've been on boats with you."

I could hear John pleading with her as I walked away.

A half hour later when we were ready to go to town, the two of them seemed to have calmed down. On the ride to shore in the Zodiac, Meg held John's knee with her left hand. I looked at Meg and she flashed me one of her dazzling smiles.

The three of us spent the afternoon and night in Portland, moving from one bar to the next. As the evening wore on, Meg became more animated — talking to whoever was nearby, laughing extravagantly at the lamest little joke. John grew increasingly sullen, staring with deep interest at whatever was in the bottom of his beer glass. I couldn't take my eyes off them. Since I knew it was only for the weekend, I sat back and took in the whole bizarre Meg-and-John show.

At about noon the next day we left our mooring and motored clear of the anchorage. John showed me how to operate the mainsail furling system. I pressed a button and the sail began to unwind from the mast. As it did, I took up on the outhaul with the winch. The sail rolled out like a big triangular window shade, even and easy.

John had Meg behind the wheel while we worked the sails. He told her to head up while we set the big genoa. When it had unfurled we began to bear away, and John showed me how to trim the sheets with the electric winches. I couldn't believe how effortless it all was. With the sail set and trimmed, *Trashman* took off, slicing through the moderate chop until we had cleared the bay. Then we bore off a little more to put her on a reach and eased off on the sails to suit the new course. She settled right into the groove.

I savored the familiar sounds of a boat under sail: the popple of the water along the leeward side, the hum of the rigging, the flutter of the back edge of the genoa. I was stationed near the winches, John was at the helm, and Meg had found a sheltered corner where she could soak up the sun and be out of the way.

After a while John bore off a bit to level the boat out while I went below to make lunch. When I came up with sandwiches and beer, we put *Trashman* on automatic pilot. A race fleet converged on a mark just off our stern, and we shouted encouragement to the leaders. Meg seemed relaxed, and John was singing along with Steve Winwood.

As soon as we decided to head back, though, everything changed. On the way out we had been reaching eastward, with the southwesterly wind on our starboard quarter. But now we had jibed and were sailing as close-hauled as we could on the port tack, heading westward. That meant we were heading almost directly into the wind and sloppy seas. Cold spray rained over the bow. We rolled up both the mainsail and the jib a little and tried to beat back up to the harbor, but it was very heavy going. The boat seemed to resist this point of sail.

I studied the sails and tried to figure out what we were doing wrong. The sails looked odd to me — they seemed stretched out and baggy — and it felt as if they were driving the boat more sideways than forward. There was no way we could get back to the harbor on one tack.

John ordered us to come about and steered *Trashman*

over to the starboard tack, but she wouldn't come around. He let her fall off to pick up speed and gave the order to try again. For some reason we couldn't get the boat to pass head to wind and onto another tack. It was as if she didn't have enough momentum to respond to the rudder. Time after time she ended up wallowing in irons or falling back onto the original tack. After a few more tries, John gave up and started the engine. That gave her the speed to complete the maneuver. So that's how we sailed back in, with the engine giving us enough of a boost to get *Trashman* to tack. I couldn't believe that a yacht of this pedigree was unable to perform such a basic maneuver under sail.

When we were still a half mile or so from our mooring, a loud alarm went off. John quickly shut down the engine.

"What's that?" Meg and I asked at the same time.

"The engine. It overheated," John said. "Take the wheel, Debbie."

John went below. Meg came over and, with some coaching, helped me operate the sheeting winches. She didn't say anything, but I could tell she was nervous. After about ten minutes, John came back up, wiping his hands with a paper towel.

"That should do it," he said.

"What was it?" Meg asked.

"The impeller. In the cooling system. I put in a spare."

John started the engine and let it idle until he was satisfied the cooling system was working again.

"Roll up that mainsail. Let's make some tracks with

this bucket," he said. He had obviously had enough fun for one day.

Our first sail had been a disappointing and disturbing one for me. John seemed tentative and, worse than that, lazy. He had refused to set the staysail or the mizzen, as most captains would have done, if only to check them out before heading offshore. And it occurred to me later that he had also neglected to lower the centerboard. No wonder she wouldn't come about. With the centerboard down, the keel would have had more bite and *Trashman* would have had something to pivot on when she tacked. Without it, we had been sliding sideways like a toy boat in a bathtub.

Other things worried me also. Some of the lines showed chafe. And the rigging on both masts was not as tight as I was accustomed to seeing, even on cruising boats. This would cause the top part of the mast to bend off to leeward, reducing the effectiveness of the sails.

As we were going to dinner that night I suggested to John, as tactfully as I could, that we might work on tuning the rigging. John told me not to worry about it. If anything had to be done, he said, we could do it once we got to Florida.

Meg left on Monday morning, just as John said she would. But a couple of days later she was back — and this time it was apparent that she planned to stay.

So now we were three. And somehow our two-day stay in Falmouth had become a week, and John gave no indication that he planned to leave soon. There were those mysterious papers, of course. But the more I thought about it, the more convinced I became that we didn't need any papers. We weren't leaving the country, for crying out loud! We were just sailing to Florida. I knew one thing for sure — I wasn't going to stay with *Trashman* once we got there.

John didn't volunteer very much information. Most mornings he would mutter something about all the errands he had to run, and he would gather up his briefcase, slap his cap on his head, and take off in the Zodiac with Meg. I welcomed a few hours of solitude — but when those hours became entire days I would get a raging case of cabin fever. I could do only so much cleaning and stowing, and the weather was so bad I couldn't varnish. Some days I'd bum a ride ashore and spend the afternoon getting quietly trashed at the boatyard bar. Other times I'd go into the restaurant, scarf down enough food for four people, then end up on my knees in a bathroom stall getting rid of it all.

Occasionally John and Meg included me on their trips to town. Meg and I would shop while John trailed along behind us like a puppy. Then we would all end up in a bar. John and Meg would fight, then make up. We'd all wake up hung over the next day.

Days went by and John still hadn't acquired the mysterious papers. I couldn't stand much more of this sitting around. Finally one evening he announced from the navigation station, "Tomorrow's the day."

Meg and I were in the main salon reading. We looked up from our books.

"We're heading out. The weather's right," he said. "Screw the papers. We're going."

✝

Trashman had just cleared Cape Elizabeth, south of Portland. We were cruising beneath a solid ceiling of slate-gray clouds. Using the mainsail more for stability than for power, we motored close-hauled into a stiff southerly wind. We expected the trip to Newport to take about twenty-four hours. John and I had decided to do alternate three-hour watches for the duration. Meg would do all the cooking and help out on deck if she was needed.

By midafternoon we were plowing through three- or four-foot seas, which *Trashman* handled fairly well. As we worked our way south, the sky cleared and the wind died. The setting sun streaked the sky orange, then magenta, then dark purple, and as the light dropped I felt a rush of joy. It was so beautiful out here and so big and so free of trouble. All the little things that had seemed important on land fell away. Out here, if you found yourself drifting off course, you could fix it with a subtle shift of the wrist.

By dawn we had motored through the Cape Cod Canal and into Buzzards Bay. A few hours later we pulled into Newport, where we found the big harbor nearly empty. John decided to spring for a berth at a dock so we could come and go without using the Zodiac. He was still talking about hiring crew, but I didn't think we'd find anybody in this ghost town. Everyone who knew how to sail and wanted to go south was probably halfway to Florida by now.

After breakfast John and Meg took off for the day in a rented car. I wandered around town, poking in some shops and walking the docks. On my way back to the boat I ran into a South African friend named Sonia, whom I had last seen a few years ago when we both were living on Virgin Gorda. She told me she was working for a Newport yacht brokerage, which happened to be the one that had sent John to see Morris Newberger about the *Trashman* job. We arranged to meet for dinner at a place called the Candy Store.

I found Sonia sitting at a small table. After we had talked for a while, I asked her what she knew about John Lippoth. She told me he had a lot of experience and that he seemed like a nice guy.

"He was on *Black Knight* before, right? What happened, exactly, with that? Why'd he get the boot?" I asked.

"Something about the girlfriend . . ."

"Meg Mooney."

"Yes. Meg Mooney. And the owners felt he just wasn't, well, working out the way they . . ."

"But what did he do?"

Someone called my name from across the bar. It was Jim, a sailing buddy I hadn't seen in months. He gave me a kiss, and I told him I'd just come in on *Trashman* with John Lippoth.

"How'd you get hooked up with him?" Jim said. "He doesn't have the best track record, you know."

"I was telling Debbie he's had a couple of little problems," Sonia said.

"Sonia helped John get the job," I said.

Jim looked surprised.

"Who's the owner?" he said.

"Guy named Newberger. He needed someone in a hurry," Sonia said. "The other people we approached wouldn't do it. The money wasn't great. We sent John to see him."

"He's probably fine," Jim said. "I really don't know the guy."

"I'm not that psyched about staying on the boat," I said. And once I had said it out loud I knew it was true. I would have been very happy to walk away right there if I thought I could find another way south.

Jim asked if we were going to take the Intracoastal Waterway.

"The mast is too tall, we'd never make it under the bridges. We'll probably go out across the Gulf Stream, then head south. Assuming we get crew, that is."

"You'll get crew in Annapolis. Try Marmaduke's. Everybody hangs out there."

✓

John and Meg were still gone when I returned to the boat. I pulled out some charts and looked at the routes we might take to Florida. I figured we'd either cross the Gulf Stream, get into deeper water, and then make a straight shot for Fort Lauderdale, or we would hug the shore all the way. Going along the coast would allow us to head into port if the weather got bad, but we would run the risk inherent in sailing shallower waters. Conditions could get very bad very quickly, and we'd have no sea room to maneuver the boat out to safety.

Since John was not big on discussing strategy, I didn't know what his plan was — or if he even had one. I suspected, though, that he would opt for the coastal route. He seemed to me the kind of sailor who took comfort in the proximity of land.

John and Meg were on board when I got up the next morning. I had understood that Meg was going to be leaving the boat here — but from the way the two of them were talking I could tell that little plan had been scratched. I said good morning and went about the business of preparing the boat to go back out to sea.

Two days later, when the wind finally shifted in our favor, we cast off in a dense fog. We'd be crossing two hundred miles of open ocean before we reached the relative shelter of Delaware Bay. Before we left, I helped John stow the Zodiac on deck. It was a relief to know that I would no longer have to keep checking on our little red friend bobbing along behind us.

We were using our now-standard rig of mainsail for stability and engine for power. In the lumpy sea outside Narragansett Bay, *Trashman* pitched a lot, and curtains of cold water sprayed up over her bow. Visibility was so low that although we passed within three miles of Block Island, we never knew it was there. But thanks to our loran navigation system, we stayed right on course.

John and I settled into a three-hours-on, three-hours-off watch schedule. Meg might as well not have been aboard; she spent almost all her time in the aft cabin. Occasionally she appeared long enough to throw together a few sandwiches or make some coffee; then she would go back to her bunk like a prairie dog running for its hole. I wondered why she wanted to be on this boat when she was so obviously unhappy at sea.

Once we cleared Long Island, the wind stiffened. I persuaded John to set the jib, and with the sail up, *Trashman* steadied herself and took off. John was so impressed he even shut down the engine. As the boat forged through the sloppy seas, the weather deteriorated. A cold wind was coming from almost astern, and the canvas and acrylic cockpit dodger offered no protection from the spray. Rain started to fall, the wind built, and within the hour we were sailing smack into what sailors everywhere know as shitty weather. The wind was not strong enough to be called a gale, the seas were not big enough to be threatening — but it was an uncomfortable and very wet ride.

Conditions became too poor to use the autopilot, so I had to take the wheel on my watch. I strained to see the lights of other ships or buoys — but there was nothing except the wind-driven rain and the dark, whipped-up sea. A little after sunrise John came up and told me we were going to head in to Cape May, New Jersey, to wait out the weather. That was fine by me. I could use a hot meal and a shower and a decent night's sleep.

The slight change in course made it difficult to keep the genoa from being blanketed by the mainsail. As the boat rolled, the genoa would collapse against the forestay and fill again with a powerful shudder. But rather than steer to the sails and correct the course as we got closer to our destination, John chose to roll up the jib and start up the engine again.

As we bashed our way through the ugly seas, John became very quiet. He even shut off Steve Winwood so he could "concentrate." I didn't know what the big deal was — I'd been in conditions much worse than these. Getting through this stuff was primarily a matter of attitude. You had to look at it as a challenge. You had to be aggressive and decisive. You had to understand that the ocean is like a snarling dog; it can sense when you are afraid.

Sometime around midmorning, when we were still an hour or so out of Cape May, the engine alarm sounded. John cursed, hit the kill button, then headed to the engine room. I was left to wrestle with the helm. Without the power of the engine or the balance provided by the jib, the boat was a bear to control. I fought with the wheel as we climbed the backs of wave after wave. The more I struggled with the steering, the angrier I got — at the boat and the weather and most of all at John, for relying so heavily on machinery, for not having the balls to just sail the boat.

John finally reappeared and said he had the engine fixed. It was the impeller again. I started to say that I thought he had "fixed" it when we were in Falmouth, but I kept my mouth shut. He started her up, and I stayed at the wheel while he went below to work with the loran. An hour later I spotted a low dark smudge of land off our starboard bow. John cheered. His precious machines were working after all — we were just where we were supposed to be.

Just outside the breakwater at the entrance to the Cape May inlet, the seas were boiling where the tide surged out of the narrow channel. As we beat our way against the current, I tried not to look at the jagged rocks that lined both sides of the passageway. If the engine quit on us now, we'd be in serious trouble. John managed to bring her through safely, and once we had docked, Meg emerged to make coffee. I poured some dark rum into mine and asked Meg and John if they wanted any. When John held his cup up I saw how badly his hand was shaking.

*

In the morning everything looked better. The seas were still rough, but nowhere near as crazy as they had been. We motored out of the channel under clear skies and headed south. Under mainsail and engine, and steering by autopilot, we had a long but relatively easy day following the shipping channels through the Chesapeake and Delaware Canal. We reached Annapolis near midnight and dropped anchor in the glassy black water. John and Meg bickered about whether or not to go out and then finally took the Zodiac ashore. I decided to stay on board. I was exhausted and I needed a break from them.

After they left, I sat on deck for a while, watching the lights of the old city dance in the dark water. There were plenty of boats around us. At last I felt that we were back in the thick of the sailing scene — maybe we'd find our elusive crew at last.

I went below to my cabin and flopped on my bunk. The palms of my hands were glazed from the leather on the steering wheel, and my body ached all over. It felt so good to press my face, hot from the sun and wind, against the cool pillow. I lay there and thought about Meg and wondered why she was with John. I thought about John and wondered why he wanted to work on boats when he didn't seem to enjoy sailing at all. I thought about my mother and wondered where she was tonight. Then I thought about Florida and sunshine and warmth. I'd be there in a few days, and none of those other things would matter.

3

Over breakfast John made it clear that the crew search
had fallen on my shoulders. From a phone on the dock I
called my friend Sarah Cavanagh, who had sailed with me
on the *Charles Heidsieck III* in the transatlantic race the
previous spring. She wasn't around, but her mother told
me that Sarah's brother, Brad, was in Annapolis and
might be interested in a job.

Two men were walking down the dock toward me.
The sandy-haired man was tall, maybe six foot three, and
extremely muscular; the blond one was short and wiry. I

realized that the tall man was Brad Cavanagh, whom I had met six months earlier.

"You won't believe this," I said, "but I just got off the phone with your mother." And then I started to tell him about *Trashman.*

"Christ, Brad, got a bird in every port, 'ave you?" the other man said. He had a British accent and the strangest pale blue eyes I had ever seen.

Brad introduced me to Mark Adams.

I asked Brad if he wanted to see *Trashman.* As the three of us walked down the dock, Mark ran into someone he knew and stopped to talk. When Brad and I got to the boat, John popped his head out of the hatch.

"Gee, Debbie, that was fast." He laughed.

"Hey, you said get crew, I got crew." I introduced him to Brad. We all went below and, after talking for a while, John asked Brad if he might want to join the crew.

"Sounds like a good possibility," Brad said. "I got this buddy Mark. Think you could use him, too?"

"Is he good?" John said.

"He's done the Fastnet, Admiral's Cup, SORC. I've done some races with him. He's kind of crazy, but he's good on a boat."

Mark came aboard and John offered him a job.

"On this pig it will probably take us a bloody year to get to Florida," Mark said, then looked at Meg and me. "These wenches aren't going, are they? I hate taking women on boats; they're absolutely useless on boats."

Everyone laughed but me. Mark told John he might

46

be able to join us even though he was busy putting together a racing crew for *Ocean Greyhound*, a big boat that had done the Whitbread a few years before.

I was surprised. I had seen that boat in dry dock in England not long before, and it seemed unlikely that it would be raced again.

"Debbie here did the last Whitbread," John said.

"That right?" Mark said.

"That's right."

"I bet I know what your job was," he said. He grabbed his crotch and shook it, then cackled. Brad reached over and gave Mark a friendly shove.

"Don't mind him, Debbie. He just likes being a prick."

I did mind him, though. I minded him very much. I got up and went on deck to find something to busy myself with. In a little while John, Mark, and Brad came up. They shook hands. It seemed to be a done deal, pending Newberger's approval, of course.

"I don't really like Mark," I said to John when I had a chance later that day.

"You don't even know him."

"I know his type."

"Brad says he's a good sailor. We need crew. He'll be on the boat for a week at most. No big deal."

John telephoned Newberger and got his okay to hire Brad and Mark, and that, of course, called for a celebration. But John's cash was running low, and he asked if any of us could loan some money to "the boat" until Newberger wired him more. Mark had a paycheck for

$150, but when the five of us walked to the marina office to cash it, the clerk looked at the check and frowned.

"Sorry, pal. Can't do it," he said.

"Come on. I'm good for it. I swear it," Mark said. "Ask anybody." Mark started reeling off names of people who could vouch for him, and the clerk finally went into the back room to call one of them. In a minute he returned and handed Mark the check.

"He said you were, quote, one of the biggest assholes he had ever met and it would be a cold day in hell before he'd cash a check of yours, unquote."

Mark's face flushed, he clenched his fists, and then he started to laugh.

"You fucking moron," he said and stormed out the door.

"I know the bartender at Marmaduke's," Mark told us. "He'll cash the bloody check."

Marmaduke's was jammed with sailors in town for the Annapolis Boat Show. Mark went off to "talk to some people about *Ocean Greyhound*." I couldn't believe he was really going to try to get people to quit their jobs to work on this fantasy project of his. This was not the way people were recruited for world-class races. I watched Mark stop and talk to someone I happened to know. When Mark moved on, my buddy waved me over.

"Are you with that guy?" he asked.

"The skipper of the boat I'm taking south just hired him," I said.

"Is he for real? He says he's hiring crew for *Ocean*

Greyhound to do the Sydney-Hobart race. It sounds like a great trip. Do you know any way to check it out? I'd really be interested."

"I've met the owner, Les Williams," I said. "Maybe I could give him a call." I looked back at John, Brad, and Meg. Mark was standing with them again, gesturing wildly, and they were laughing so hard they were doubled over. Maybe it's just me, I thought. Maybe he's really a prince of a guy.

I turned in early, but I had trouble falling asleep. I couldn't stop thinking about Mark and *Ocean Greyhound*. In the morning, before anyone else was up, I went to the pay phone and called a friend who told me how to reach Les Williams in England. When the call went through I explained who I was and said I had just been asked by Mark Adams to join the crew of *Ocean Greyhound*.

He told me the boat was still in dry dock and that he had never heard of Mark Adams. So I had my answer. I felt kind of sick, almost wishing I hadn't made the call. I knew for certain that Mark was not just annoying, he was a liar. I sat down on the dock and stared into the metallic blue water and tried to decide what to do. I couldn't believe this whole thing: this wild, belligerent Englishman, this half-assed skipper, and his ball-busting nonsailing girlfriend. It was a joke.

I sat and thought for a few more minutes. What if I just get my gear and walk away now? I have friends in Annapolis. I'll find another way south. No, that's dumb. Why should I leave my boat? I decided I had to tell John what I had found out about Mark. When he heard about it he would have to kick Mark off *Trashman*, wouldn't he?

"You know the *Ocean Greyhound* crew Mark says he's hiring?" I said to John later that morning. "It's all bullshit. The owner never heard of him."

"How would you know that?" he asked.

"I made a call to England."

"You what? Oh God, Debbie, I really don't want to hear about it. I don't care what this guy is doing or not doing, okay? We need crew. He's crew. That's it. Why don't you just mind your own business for once."

"This *is* my business. I don't want to sail with that guy. I don't want to go if he's going."

"That's ridiculous."

"I'm serious. I'll leave the boat."

"If you leave this boat now," John said slowly, "I will make damn sure that you never get a job on another boat again. I mean it. You can't just get off the boat just like that."

"I can, John. I'm not your little slave. I don't want to go with Mark."

"Debbie. For the last time — you are not getting off this boat. We are going to provision the boat tomorrow, and then we are going to leave the next day. All of us. You, me, Meg, Brad, and Mark."

"I understand how you feel about Mark," Meg said. She had been listening to our conversation. "But if you just ignore him . . ."

"Yeah, just ignore the guy," John said.

"And it would help if you stuck up for Debbie once in a while," Meg said to John.

He sighed. "Look. Once we get under way everything will be great. You'll see," he said and went up on deck.

But I couldn't let it go. I had had enough. As soon as I could get away, I walked back to the pay phone and called Morris Newberger. I told him that I had changed my mind, that I missed racing and was going to fly south and try to get a job on a racing boat. Newberger asked if there was a problem with the rest of the crew. I hesitated and then said no, no problem, really. When he began to remind me of my commitment, I could feel my resolve weakening. Before his lecture was over, I knew that I was not going to get out of this trip. I was going south with *Trashman*. I walked back to the boat feeling like a fool — for making the call and for being such a pushover.

1

By five o'clock John, Meg, Brad, and I had everything stowed, cleaned, and checked over. We got cleaned up and headed to a restaurant to meet Mark and have one last celebration before our departure. We ate dinner, then moved to the bar just as Mark came lurching in.

"This is Tilly," Mark said, losing his balance and almost knocking over the small, pretty, brown-haired girl he was trying to introduce us to. John reached out to keep him from tipping over.

After ordering more drinks, Mark stumbled toward me.

"Hey, Mark," I said, "I just talked to a friend of mine in England today. Les Williams, the guy who owns *Ocean Greyhound?*"

Everyone stopped talking, and Mark's face turned red.

"He said he never heard of you," I went on. "He said his boat was in pieces."

"You stupid cunt," he snarled, bringing his face close to mine. "What the fuck are you doing checking up on me?"

"No big deal," I said. "He seemed surprised, that's all."

"Come on, guys," John said. "We're having a good time here. Don't wreck it."

"I'm not wrecking anything," I said. "I'm having a great time."

"You think you're so fucking special, Miss Whitbread," Mark said.

Brad reached over and grabbed Mark under the armpit. "Come on," he said. "Sit down here. Forget about it. Debbie, just drop it, okay?"

"Fine," I said.

As we were leaving after last call, Mark grabbed a full bottle of Dewar's from behind the bar and bolted for the door. Back on *Trashman*, we partied until almost dawn. Mark, who was drinking Dewar's straight from the bottle, brought the party to an abrupt end by reaching up under Tilly's skirt and pulling down her underwear. Mortified, Tilly went back to her boat, and the rest of us headed for our cabins. I was drunk and tired and disgusted with Mark.

1

By noon we were ready to cast off. The crew was in rough shape, but the weather was great. The wind was behind us from the north-northwest at 10 to 15 knots under clear skies, and the temperature was in the high sixties. We had run a weather fax that morning and listened to the radio reports, and it looked as if we would have good weather for the next three or four days. We took off down the Chesapeake using the mizzen, the main, and the multi-purpose sail. *Trashman* loved it. She was flying, surfing down waves at 9 knots and making us forget what a big, heavy boat she was.

The wind began to build late in the afternoon. Just before sunset, John decided to take down the multipurpose. He said he didn't want to risk damaging Newberger's prize possession in the dark. About six o'clock we started our watch rotation. Mark and John took the first stint, and Brad and I went below to sleep.

Three hours later, Meg woke us for dinner. John had put the boat on automatic pilot so we could all sit down together. Meg, John, and Brad were in good spirits, but Mark sat stone-faced, staring at me with those glacier-blue eyes.

"If you think I've forgotten about you checking up on me, little Miss Whitbread, you're wrong," he finally said. "Paybacks are a bitch. You'll see."

I looked at John. He was the skipper. It was his job to keep the crew in line.

"Keep it to yourself, man," John said.

After a moment of tense silence, Meg started chattering about some bar in Fort Lauderdale she wanted to see, and everyone seemed to relax again. I finished my dinner quickly and went up on deck. It was a beautiful starry night, and *Trashman* was dancing across the waves. I tried to forget about Mark and concentrate on the wonderful sound of the boat slicing cleanly through the water. I closed my eyes and let the wind hit my face. The air was chilly, but I was dressed for it. And I knew that with every minute we were that much closer to Florida.

When Brad came on deck we took the autopilot off. With the wind just off the stern, *Trashman* was in full sail, wing and wing, with the main and the mizzen and the jib poled out. It was the first time I'd sailed her like this, and she felt fantastic.

Brad and I took turns at the helm and talked, enjoying ourselves so much we decided to let the others sleep a little longer. I liked Brad — he was easygoing and funny and obviously in love with sailing. There was a gentleness about him that belied his size. He reminded me of a giant teddy bear. He told me how he had grown up in a suburb north of Boston, and his father had started him sailing when he was just a little kid.

"When my mother was pregnant with me, she and my father sailed through a hurricane," Brad said. "And when I was in high school my dad had a thirty-eight-footer that I was required to sail on every weekend —"

54

"Required?"

"Yeah. Every weekend and every day when my father was on vacation."

I told him I had learned to sail at summer camp in Texas, but I hadn't been around boats again until I dropped out of college in Austin and took off for the Caribbean.

"Wasn't your mother pissed off that you quit school?" Brad asked.

"I didn't tell her," I said. "I just left. I called four months later. I don't think she even knew I was gone."

Around four in the morning we stopped talking and realized how tired we were. After we got John and Mark to come up and take their watch, I collapsed in my bunk and almost instantly fell asleep.

*

Four hours later, when I came on deck for my next watch, I was happy to see that we had left the mouth of the bay and were heading out into open ocean. The conditions were still wonderful, with brisk 15- to 20-knot winds, a light chop, and a few puffy clouds.

When I went below to get coffee, I saw John at the navigation station. I asked him whether we were still planning to rendezvous with Tilly's boat in Beaufort, North Carolina, to celebrate her birthday.

"I think with the forecast so good we should just keep going," John said. "Be just my luck to get into Beaufort and get stuck there for a week with shitty weather. Anyway, I can't find that chart."

"What chart?"

"The chart for that whole coast. Doesn't really matter. We won't need it."

I went back up and took the helm from Brad. We had changed our course slightly and were heading a little more to the southeast in order to get seaward of Cape Hatteras. I had never sailed the Atlantic Coast before, but I knew the area was notorious for rough weather. We were still on the same tack and broad-reaching with the main, mizzen, and jib. Sometime during their watch, Mark and John had taken the pole off the jib. We were still moving well, and I started to think we might just get to Florida sooner than expected.

Around noon, John and Mark came on deck, each drinking a beer. Mark was carrying a small plastic cooler.

"Want a cold one?" Mark asked Brad, who shook his head.

After a quick lunch, Brad and I went back to our bunks. When I woke up around four in the afternoon, I could tell from the way the boat was riding that the wind had picked up. I put on my foul-weather gear, woke Brad, and went on deck. The wind was blowing 25 to 30 knots, the seas had built to about 10 to 12 feet, and a bank of dark clouds was advancing from the horizon. The weather fax hadn't indicated any change, but something seemed to be blowing up.

Mark and John had rolled up the jib, main, and mizzen about 25 percent. We were still on a port tack, moving along quite well even through the bigger seas. Brad and I traded off the helm every twenty minutes or so, and each time I took the wheel I had to work harder to keep *Trashman* on course. By the end of our four-hour watch the wind had stiffened to about 30 to 35 knots and the seas were rolling in at 12 to 15 feet.

Down below, the Steve Winwood tape finished rewinding and started playing again.

"We have to get John to change that tape," I said. "I can't take it anymore."

When I went down to get John and Mark for their watch, I found them sitting in the main cabin.

"Thirsty?" John asked and held up a beer.

"What did the last weather fax say?" I asked while I peeled off my foul-weather gear.

"Same thing as the last one and the one before that." John shrugged.

"It's getting rough," I said.

"That's not rough," Mark said as he climbed up the companionway, trying not to spill the amber liquid in his glass.

"I think I will have something. What's he drinking?" I said.

"Dewar's."

"And what?"

"Just Dewar's."

I made myself a vodka and cranberry juice and collapsed on the settee. My face was hot from windburn, and my skin was gritty with salt. Brad came down and got himself a beer, and we ate the lasagna Meg had heated up. Then we went back to our bunks to get some sleep.

✔

I could feel someone shaking my arm.

"Get up, Debbie. Right now." It was John, and his voice sounded tight.

"I'm up," I said.

"What's going on?" Brad asked.

"It's blowing thirty-five to forty, but none of the weather reports indicate any change. It's really bizarre, man. It's a fuckin' gale out of nowhere."

I sat up. "What's the sail situation?"

"We've reduced sail as much as we can with this stupid roller-furling rig. We rolled the jib all the way in, and we've got the club-foot staysail up. We rolled up the main another twenty-five percent . . . so we've got about half of it out now."

The boat slammed over a wave and shuddered.

"Shit," John said.

"What about the mizzen?" Brad asked.

"We rolled that up an hour ago."

Out on deck the weather didn't seem nearly as bad as John had made it out to be. The seas had built, but we were in the Gulf Stream, after all, where conditions were always magnified. And a low-pressure area just north of the Bahamas was probably kicking up a sizable ocean swell from the east. I thought probably conditions would stay pretty messy until we got across the Stream.

I took the helm, then traded with Brad after about ten minutes. It was going to be that kind of watch — short stints of hard work alternating with short rest breaks. After a while John came to the foot of the companionway and called up.

"I think I want to jibe now," he said.

Brad and I exchanged looks of disbelief.

"Here? Now?" I yelled down to John. "What's up — you decide to go to Tilly's birthday party?"

"I'm worried about the weather. I don't want to get caught in the Gulf Stream if this gets any worse."

"I got news for you, bro," Brad said. "I think we're already in it."

"Then we're going to get back just inside of it and stay there."

This didn't make much sense to me. Even though the Gulf Stream could be treacherous, we were awfully close to Cape Hatteras to be thinking about heading toward shore. Still, it was John's call. Brad and I jibed the boat.

On the starboard tack the wind was almost dead astern and gusting up to 40 knots. I hoped to God John knew what he was doing. Brad and I traded turns at the helm. Every time I got back to the wheel the seas seemed to have gotten more chaotic, the wind more powerful. It was exhausting trying to keep the boat on course, and by midnight, when our watch ended, I was desperate for sleep.

Below, the two big chairs were sliding back and forth with every heave of the boat, digging deep scars into the polished floor. I asked John if he wanted me to secure them, but he said not to bother. I was relieved — I barely had the energy to take off my foul-weather gear and crash.

Four hours later, Brad and I were back on deck and the weather had definitely gotten uglier. We sailed more and talked less as our watch went on, and by the time it ended, we were both spent.

✔

"Let's go," I heard John say.

I groaned and rubbed my eyes.

"Was that four hours?"

"It's really nasty out there," he said. "We're taking on some water."

I rubbed my eyes again.

"C'mon, you got to get up there quick," John said impatiently. "Mark's . . . kind of wild. We have to get him down."

John said he was going to work on the generator — he wanted to have it ready in case we needed extra power. I pulled on my wet gear, thinking that John was just not used to dealing with weather. Then I felt the boat being lifted stern first, as if it were on a hoist. I reached out to steady myself as the boat listed and groaned. We paused for a split second, and I felt that suspended agony you feel on a roller coaster as it crests a steep hill. Then we started down and my stomach seemed to drop away.

"Holy shit," Brad said. I heard Mark hollering up on deck. *Trashman*'s hull shuddered violently as we tore down the face of the wave with unbelievable speed. I reached out for the bulkhead to keep from falling backward, then pulled myself toward the companionway.

When I got up on deck and saw Mark at the helm, I froze. He was laughing, talking to himself, howling into the wind. His white-blond hair was plastered against his scalp, and with his electric green sweater, red face, and pale eyes, he looked like a creature from another planet.

Brad came up behind me. "Holy shit," he said again as he stared at Mark and the mountainous seas. The wind had to be blowing 45, 50, maybe 55 knots, and the seas were walls of liquid granite thirty or thirty-five feet high. Solid water crashed onto our stern. I went for the helm, and Mark stepped aside, lost his balance, and landed with a thud on the sole of the cockpit.

"Man overboard," he said with a laugh, dropping his chin to his chest. He was drunk — falling-down drunk. He crawled to the companionway.

" 'ope it's not too rough for you, Miss Whitbread," he said as he lowered himself down the hatch.

"Go fuck yourself, Mark," I said.

"Go fuck yourself, Mark," he repeated in a high-pitched whine from below.

4.

Once I had the helm and felt the boat careening down the enormous waves, I could see why Mark had been hollering like a maniac. It took all my strength to hold the rudder against the tremendous force of the water. I had seen seas like this on *Xargo*, but I had never steered through them myself. It was terrifying and thrilling and way beyond anything I had ever experienced on a boat.

Brad called down to tell John he thought we should get the cockpit dodger down before we lost it. John popped his head up and talked to Brad for a minute, then disappeared.

"He says he can't find the boards that go in the companionway," Brad said. "If we take the dodger down, the shutters will let in too much spray." The rigging was vibrating so loudly I could hardly hear what he was saying.

Brad offered to take the helm, and I dropped down next to him and stared at the sea. It was all peaks and valleys; there were no straight lines beyond the railing of our boat. And everything was gray. Was this the gray of dawn or noon or dusk? I had to stop and think for a minute. Did it matter? I had a vision of what this scene must look like from above, the waves rearing up behind the stern like ferocious animals, ready to pounce.

When we flew down into the dark canyons between waves, the wind quit and the noise stopped, as if someone had thrown a switch on a simulated storm. Then the wild ride would start again and we would be hauled back up into the raging seas. I didn't know which was worse, the creepy quiet of the trough or the howling fury of the crest.

Through the din I heard Meg calling my name. I was startled by the sound of her voice. I hadn't seen her for what, a day? I felt myself getting angry at John all over again for bringing her along. What good was she? In this weather we could have used a capable extra hand. When Meg asked if Brad or I wanted coffee, I realized I hadn't had any breakfast.

I found Meg standing in the galley wearing one of

John's button-down oxford shirts and a pair of purple sweatpants.

"Pretty rough out there, huh?" she said, handing me coffee. The boat pitched and I tried to keep the cup steady.

"How would you know?" I said. "Been on deck lately?"

Meg's eyes registered her hurt, and she looked away. "Please don't bitch at me, Debbie. You know I wouldn't be any help up there — oh, my God." The boat was free-falling again; Meg lost her balance, slammed across the cabin, and landed against the settee. I managed to stay on my feet and went over to help her up.

"Are you all right?" I asked.

"I'm fine," she said and jerked away from my hand.

"I'm sorry," I said. "I'm just wiped out."

There was a loud crash on deck and Brad started screaming. I rushed back up and found him staring wide-eyed at the stern.

"Are you okay?" I asked.

"It's gone."

"What's gone?"

I turned to see what he was looking at and realized that the Dyer Dhow dinghy had been swept away. All that remained on board was a piece of one of the davits.

"What happened?"

"One wave. Just took it, like, bam!" Brad said. "I didn't see it coming."

John came up. When he saw that we had lost the dinghy, he shook his head slowly.

65

"Oh, man, Newberger's going to shit," he said. He stared at the empty place where the dinghy had hung. "He's going to kill me."

At noon our watch ended and I went to sleep. Four hours later, Brad and I were back on deck and conditions were no better. If anything, the wind had intensified and the waves had become more monstrous. The club foot on the staysail had broken sometime in the afternoon when a wave hit and caused the boat to jibe. The staysail had been vanged down, and the pressure from the jibe, coupled with the water sweeping across the deck, had been too much for it. Luckily the sail itself hadn't been damaged.

Once I had the helm I saw how hard it was to control the staysail. And now that it was getting dark, steering the boat would be even more daunting because we wouldn't be able to see what we were fighting. I told myself that the situation was still manageable. We just have to keep cool, do what needs to be done, Brad and I kept saying to each other. But by the time our watch ended at eight we couldn't hide our exhaustion — or our fear. When I got below I saw Meg pulling on her foul-weather gear. I asked her what she was doing.

"Going up to help."

"Are you kidding? It's a nightmare up there." She shrugged and climbed the stairs. I was too tired to think about Meg now. I watched her go and went back to my cabin.

Some time later I was awakened by John. He was leaning over me and shaking my shoulders and talking so fast I could barely understand him.

"We got problems. Meg fell and hurt her back. I got to get to the engine room to try and get the generator going, and I can't leave Mark up there by himself."

Brad sat up and started pulling on his gear. "What happened to her?"

John said Meg had unsnapped the tether on her safety harness before coming back down. Just as she unsnapped it, a wave hit and knocked her to the other side of the cockpit.

"She has this huge bruise," John said. "It looks bad."

I found Meg on the floor of the aft cabin lying amidships with her feet braced against one of the bunks. Every time the boat heaved she winced in pain, but when I asked what I could do she insisted she was all right. I poked my head into the engine room to see how John was coming with the generator. It was quiet in there, almost peaceful, despite the violent lurching of the boat. John was sitting on the floor drinking a beer.

"Having a party in here?" I said.

"How's Meg?"

"She says she's okay. What are you doing?"

"I'm thinking."

"I thought you were working on the generator."

"I am. I'm thinking about it."

"Oh."

"You better get on deck," John said.

I couldn't believe he was sitting there, dry and warm,

drinking a beer — and telling me to hurry and get up on deck. I found Brad at the helm with Mark sitting next to him.

"Oh, thank you, Sheesus, we're saved," Mark said. "Miss Whitbread is 'ere."

"Are you out of your mind?" I screamed at him. "We're in a gale and you're shit-faced. You are a bigger asshole than I thought."

"Quit whining," Mark said and struggled to his feet. "She's still fuckin' floating, isn't she?"

He reeled toward the companionway.

"He's going to get us all killed!" I shouted at Brad.

"What do you want me to do?" Brad shouted back. "He was up here with the skipper, for Christ's sake. What am I supposed to do about it?"

When I took the helm I had to forget about Mark — forget about everything but trying to control the boat. With sustained winds close to 60 knots it was almost impossible to keep the staysail from jibing. When we were on top of a wave we were all right. But as soon as we dropped into a trough, the wind was blanketed, and the cross seas pushed the boat sideways, causing the sails to flap wildly. One strong jibe and our mast could snap. It was getting far too dangerous to keep carrying the mainsail, but we were stuck with it. We hadn't been able to roll the last 25 percent of the sail into the mast, and it would have been almost suicidal to try to take it down now.

It took everything I had to keep *Trashman* upright. When I was at the helm I was so focused I didn't have time to be afraid. But when Brad had the wheel, I could see what hell we were sailing through. Incredibly, the wind and seas kept building. The anemometer read 66, 67, 68, then moved to 71. The mainmast was vibrating so intensely it felt as if it might shake the boat apart. By 4 A.M., I was totally wiped out. Brad went below to get Mark and John, but he came back without them.

"John says he needs a little more time with the generator. And Mark's passed out. I can't wake him up."

"This is great. How long does it take to fix a generator?"

"We can go a little longer. Give me the wheel. You go get us some coffee."

John was coming from the aft cabin when I got below. He asked if I could go back and talk to Meg again.

"Just try to make her feel better about the weather, you know? Tell her everything is cool."

Oh, right, I wanted to scream. Everything's cool. Maybe he'd like me to tell her about the moonlight dancing on the quiet water or the sweet breeze kissing our sails. How about, hey, Meg, the waves look like the fucking Himalayas and I'm scared shitless and you should be too. Meg was still lying on the floor. She had been crying.

"How you guys doing up there?" she said.

"It's not much fun, but we're hanging in. How about you?" I asked. She looked awful.

"I'll be okay when we get there."

After talking to her for a few more minutes, I went back on deck. A short time later John came up and told us he wanted to turn on the engine.

"Now?" Brad said.

"I'm worried about Meg," he said. "We need to get her to a hospital."

"I don't know how much more speed we're going to get," Brad said.

"I've got to charge the batteries anyway," John said.

Brad turned the key and pressed the button, and the engine kicked on. Steve Winwood came blaring out of the speakers. Brad and I continued to take turns at the helm as our watch dragged on and on. When we had been on deck for almost six hours, Brad went below again to try to get Mark and John to take over.

Brad returned alone. "John said he needed a few more minutes with the generator, and Mark is still out cold."

At that moment the engine alarm sounded, and John came racing up on deck. He pushed me out of the way and killed the motor.

"I don't fucking believe this shit!" he said. "What else can go wrong? We must have burned up another impeller."

"So we'll fix it," Brad said. "Take it easy."

"I don't know if there's another one on board." John raked his hands through his hair and swore again. "Can you come help me look?"

*

The light of a storm-dulled dawn leaked into the eastern sky. I had heard things breaking and groaning and ripping through the night — now I could see the damage that had been done. *Trashman* had been ravaged. The dodger was shredded, the anemometer torn off. One of the antennas had disappeared, and part of the radar had been sheared away. Only the Zodiac, lashed to the deck, seemed unscathed. All of a sudden I felt very alone. I called Brad's name. No answer. I hollered again and again, and finally Mark came up through the hatch.

"Quit your bloody shriekin'. What's your problem?"

"What's my problem? My problem is that I want you and John to get your butts up here right now to stand your watch."

"John's busy. He's looking for something with Brad."

Mark dropped back into the cabin, and I was alone again.

"Brad!"

In a few minutes Brad came up with John. They hadn't been able to find another impeller, and John still couldn't locate the coastal chart for Cape Hatteras, so even if we wanted to head for shore we had no way of setting a course. He had also discovered that the centerboard was jammed; he couldn't get it up or down.

"You mean it has been down the whole time?" I asked.

"I just told you, it's stuck halfway," John said.

"Well, there's got to be a way to move it manually," I said.

"I don't know."

"There's always a way."

"How do you know?"

"I just know, John," I said.

"Debbie, maybe there isn't a way on this boat," Brad said.

"There's always —"

"Debbie, be quiet for a minute, will ya?" John said. "The bottom line is we have to get Meg to a hospital. I'm going to call the Coast Guard and get a course to the nearest port."

"How do you think we are going to get into a harbor without an engine?" I said. "Don't you think we'd be better off just riding it out? It's not like Meg is in any danger —"

"Who is the skipper on this boat?" John said angrily. "It's me, all right? Me. And I am calling the Coast Guard."

"Shit," I said after John went below.

"I know, but what are you going to do?" Brad said.

At six-thirty in the morning, Brad took the helm from me. We had been on watch for six and a half hours, and conditions were still getting worse. I slid back the hatch and stuck my head below. The cabin was a wreck. The two chairs were lying on their sides, their cushions soaked. Everything that wasn't nailed down was shifting with each violent heave of the boat.

John was on the radio, talking to the Coast Guard.

"I gave them our position," John said when he finished.

"And?"

"And I told them we had an injured person on board and that she required medical attention and that I needed a course. They said to stand by."

The radio crackled with static. The Charleston Coast Guard was calling back with a course for John to steer. We both went up on deck to tell Brad our new heading.

"I don't know if we can do that," Brad said. "It's going to put us broadside to the waves."

"Just do it, man," John said wearily and went below.

Brad struggled to bring the boat up to meet the new course, but with only the staysail and a small triangle of mainsail we were almost dead in the water. Wave after wave pummeled our starboard side.

"We can't do this," Brad said. "I'm bringing her back down. Go tell John."

Turning, I saw Mark standing by the hatch.

"What the hell are you yabboes doing out here? Can't you keep this tub on a course?"

"Shut up, Mark," Brad snapped. It was the first time I had heard him speak that way to Mark. "Go get John. And why don't you check your fucking watch while you're at it. You have any idea what time it is?"

Mark glared at Brad, then went below.

"Why does he have to be such an asshole?" I asked. "I just can't believe —"

"Debbie, stop. Just stop. I am so sick and tired of you two bitching at each other all the time. Just shut up for one minute, you know? You think you can do that?"

Stung by Brad's words, I reached for the wheel.

"Move over. It's my turn," I said coldly. Brad stepped aside and went down the companionway without saying another word.

I decided to try bringing *Trashman* back to the Coast Guard's 300-degree course. I could feel the enormous pressure on the rudder as I steered her, but if I cracked off the course just a hair I could maintain enough speed to keep the waves from mauling our starboard quarter. It wasn't 300 degrees, but it wasn't far off — and we were making headway. It probably wasn't going to get us where John wanted to go, but trying to get into any harbor seemed suicidal. We had had enough trouble getting into Cape May with engine power and only 35 knots of wind. John was crazy to think he could do it in this.

Brad came back up to tell me they were going to put the Lexan storm shutters over the cabin windows, and I'd have to handle the helm by myself.

"I can't do it anymore, Brad," I said, fighting back tears. "I'm too tired. You tell John or Mark to get up here right now."

In a couple of minutes Mark appeared. He didn't say a word to me, just took the wheel. I felt dizzy and weak. I thought I might pass out. When I made my way down to the main salon, I heard John on the radio again, setting up a schedule for hourly radio communication with the Coast Guard. The clock said 8:20 A.M. I had been on watch for nearly eight and a half hours.

John got off the radio and asked me to help Brad find the window covers. I took a deep breath. All I wanted to do was sleep, but I knew I had to help. I found Brad digging through gear in the forepeak. We looked for twenty minutes, but we still couldn't find the last shutter.

I could hear Mark shouting from the cockpit. "Someone better bloody well come right now! I'm not staying up here by myself. Either get up here now or I'm going to lash the helm and come down."

Brad said he would go up for a few minutes if John

promised to relieve him soon. Water cascaded through the hatch as Brad climbed up. The boat shimmied and moaned as it hurtled down the face of a wave. We landed hard, and all three of us fell against the walls. I heard Meg scream in pain from the aft cabin.

"That's it," John said. He crossed to the navigation station, turned on the radio, and began trying to raise the Charleston Coast Guard. After two attempts, he got a reply.

"I know I'm calling a little early, but I think I'm going to have to ask you for assistance," John said. "We are really getting beat up good out here. The hull's down in the water and things really don't look too good right now. Over."

Hearing John admit defeat frightened me. I had never been on a boat that had requested Coast Guard assistance. I felt a confusing rush of humiliation and relief. I went up and told Mark and Brad that John had just radioed for help.

"No way," Mark said. "We're fine. We don't need the bloody Coast Guard. Fuckin' amateurs."

John came on deck and told Mark he'd take over the helm. Mark sat down in the cockpit next to Brad.

"Fuckin' amateurs," he mumbled again.

✦

When I went down to check on Meg, I found her asleep on the floor. She looked as if she hadn't moved in ten hours. I wondered if she had even gone to the bathroom. Seeing her like that filled me with a rush of guilt. I worried that she had gone up on deck because I had taunted her — and now here she was, hurt. We slammed into a wave, and I fell against the door frame. Then I worked my way forward. John was calling me, and I joined the rest of the crew in the cockpit.

"I want to make a sail change," John said. "The stay-sail's ripped. I want to try letting out just enough of the genoa to give us a little stability. And we're going to let out a little more of the main — we've got to get some speed."

Mark stood with his arms folded, shaking his head. John ignored him, and in a minute Mark went below, still muttering to himself. Brad and I got busy carrying out John's orders. Suddenly, as I was bending over, I saw Mark burst up the companionway and lunge at John. He was holding a winch handle over his head and was about to bring it down on John's head. I screamed and John ducked.

"What are you doing?" I shouted at Mark. He turned toward me and brought the handle back over his shoulder again. Then he reached out with his free hand, grabbed my arm, and twisted it hard. Brad dragged Mark off me, then Mark turned toward the water and brought his arm back again as if to throw the winch handle overboard. Brad twisted the handle out of Mark's hand, and Mark pulled away and stormed down the companionway.

"He's insane," I said in disbelief.

"He's shit-faced," John said. "Forget him. We have to do this now."

John went to the leeward side, where the staysail was sheeted, and began to ease off the sheet while I pulled in the furling line. When John took the new sheet to the genoa and wrapped it around the winch, I moved to the starboard side and began uncoiling the furling line for the genoa. I knew if I wasn't careful, the wind could catch the sail and pull it all the way out. I eased the line around the winch and let it out slowly as John brought the sheet in. And then, in a flash, my worst fears came true and the entire genoa was flying out in front of the boat, flapping thunderously. *Trashman* was being pulled over onto her side. The furling line had snapped. When John saw the sail take off, he immediately released the sheet, and the boat righted itself.

"We have to get it down!" John shouted. If the sail got caught under the hull, it could drag the boat down with it. John worked his way out to the bow, fighting to keep from being washed overboard by the waves raking the deck.

I crawled to the mainmast and wrapped one leg around it. The wire-rope jib halyard was corroded onto the reel winch, and when I finally was able to force it off, I motioned to John to pull the sail down. He gave a couple of strong tugs. Nothing happened. I looked up and saw that the head of the sail had been blown right out of the groove that held it to the forestay.

After taking several wraps on the winch and locking the halyard down, I made my way back to the cockpit, struggling to keep my feet under me as water swept across the boat. We desperately needed another pair of hands, even if they were Mark's. I ducked down through the hatch and saw Mark talking on the radio.

"— not that bad," he was saying. "I'm just dealing with a bunch of yabboes."

"Mark, get off the radio. We need you up here now. We have to get a sail down." I went back up and tried to figure out how to get to John. He was still at the bow, but the leeward side of the boat was now completely underwater.

"What the hell —" I heard Brad say. When I looked up I saw Mark bursting out of the hatch with a butcher knife in his teeth. He took it out of his mouth and started waving it in the air, shouting, "Idiots! Just cut it down, cut it down. You're going to get us all killed!"

I worked my way toward John, clipping my safety harness from one anchor point to the next. Just as I reached him, a wave collapsed on us. We clutched at each other and the sail. When the water had subsided, we counted to three, then pulled as hard as we could. I felt the sail move a little. Another wave engulfed us and we waited, then pulled again, harder, and the sail came billowing down on top of us.

Water swept across the bow, and suddenly I was floating in folds of Dacron. I felt myself being dragged to the leeward side of the boat. My hand hit something solid. I gripped it and pulled myself out of the sail and back toward the cockpit. When I looked back, John was still engulfed in the sail, trying to haul it on deck.

"Let it go, John!" I screamed. He was going to die saving a sail. A wave knocked me over and washed me to the leeward lifeline. I gasped for air and clawed my way up. Then, somehow, John surfaced next to me.

"Keep going before the next one hits," he shouted. Water poured down on me again, and I was sliding. Then I felt someone grab my foul-weather gear and drag me into the cockpit. It was Mark.

"What the fuck are you guys doing? Why can't you just leave things alone! You're gonna get us all killed, for Christ's sake!" He had put the knife down.

The air was so full of spray it was hard to see and hard to breathe. The four of us sat in the cockpit, hanging on for dear life as the boat yawed and pitched and dove. Mark buried his face in his hands. I took the helm while John and Brad began securing the shutters over the three starboard cabin windows. The port side of the boat, including the windows, was completely under water, so even if we had found all the shutters, we never would have been able to attach them.

I continued to steer the boat, although steering is not an accurate description of what I was doing. It was all I could do to hold the wheel as we rode over the mountains and charged into the valleys. My arms were shaking with fatigue, and my hands were so raw and red and cold I had lost all feeling in them. When the starboard shutters were finally secured, John went below and Brad took the helm. Mark came into the cockpit and said John was on the radio with the Coast Guard.

"I think they said they're sending a plane," Mark said.

Brad and I laughed out loud at the thought of it — a plane flying out here to find us. It seemed ridiculous, but

Mark insisted that was what they had said. I looked up at the low, smudged sky. What could a plane do for us now? Maybe airlift Meg — or all of us — off the boat? But that would mean abandoning *Trashman,* and I couldn't see us doing that.

Meg came to the companionway. I was surprised to see her moving around. She said a plane was headed out to us, and we should holler when we heard it. That way John could tell the pilot when he was getting close. What with the roar of the wind, the crashing of the waves, and the whine of the vibrating rigging, I didn't know how we'd be able to hear it, but sure enough, in just a few minutes we heard an engine. John stuck his head up through the hatch.

"See anything yet? They think they're right over us. Let me know as soon as you see them."

I looked up and waited. Like a dream, a small twin-engine prop plane emerged from the low clouds. I banged on the hatch and called John. Brad, Mark, and I waved and shouted and laughed. It seemed so crazy, so unreal, as if some great mythical bird had swooped down out of the heavens to snatch us from our hell.

"Ever see an albatross, Brad?" I shouted without taking my eyes off the plane.

"No," he said, watching the plane make a slow circle.

"They're incredible. I saw one in the Southern Ocean. It was blowing stink just like now, and this huge bird appeared out of nowhere and hung over us. They're supposed to be good luck."

The plane disappeared for a moment in the low clouds, and when it reappeared we all waved again. Then it dipped a wing and went back into the overcast. I could hear John on the radio. The Coast Guard said two merchant vessels were near us — the *Gypsum King* and the *Exxon Huntington*. They had been advised of our situation and were going to try to rendezvous with us. They were about five and a half hours away, which meant that one or both of them would be here sometime around four-thirty in the afternoon. Okay, I thought. We can hang on until then.

The rush of seeing the plane wore off, and I realized how tired I was after being on deck for almost eleven hours. Brad and I left Mark at the helm. He seemed to have sobered up somewhat, and since we had finally managed to manually furl the entire mainsail and were under bare poles, there wasn't much he could screw up.

John had put the EPIRB, an emergency transmitter that can send distress signals to passing planes and ships, on the chart table. The radio had been turned off to conserve power and wouldn't be turned on until we made our next contact with the Coast Guard about noon.

All we could do now was wait and try to get some sleep. I headed back to the cabin and peeled off my layers of clothing. The only dry clothes I had left were an old red sweatshirt and a pair of striped nylon running shorts. I put them on and climbed into my bunk. It was damp, but I didn't care. I heard water pouring through the louvered shutters in the companionway. Then I heard the thump of the bilge pump kicking on. The ships were probably four hours away now. If I could just sleep for four hours, help would be here. Just as I was dozing off, Mark started hollering.

"I'm not staying up here by myself! Somebody better bloody well get up here or I'm lashing the helm. I'm gonna lash the fuckin' helm."

Not my problem, I thought. Not my problem.

5

"Come on! We're going!"

Someone was screaming, jolting me out of a deep sleep. Was it time to go on watch again? I felt as if I'd just closed my eyes.

"We're going! Now!" It was Brad. He had me by the arm and was dragging me out of my bunk. When my feet hit the floor, I was almost up to my knees in water.

"Go!" Brad shouted and pushed me toward the galley.

What was going on? Why was he pushing me? Then I understood: the Coast Guard must have come, or one of the merchant ships. Staggering toward the main cabin, I heard a strange rushing noise, as if the ship were right on top of us. And then I saw water cascading into the cabin through the port-side windows. My God, had they hit us? Had they smashed the windows? I saw Mark splashing through the rising water, coughing, his eyes huge. Then Meg was in the doorway, rigid with shock. She opened her mouth to scream, but no sound came out.

"Come on, Meg!!" Brad yelled. John came up behind her, glanced at the flooding cabin, and shoved Meg forward toward the companionway. Then he lunged for the radio as Brad pushed me toward the stairs.

"Mayday. . . mayday. . . we're sinking, we're sunk —" John was hollering. Why bother with the radio when the ship is already here? I wondered. We didn't have time to screw around; the water was nearly shoulder deep.

I crawled up the companionway behind Brad, fighting to keep my balance as the boat hurtled down the face of a wave. We both made it to the deck. But where was the ship? Where were the people who had come to rescue us? There was nothing, only the monster seas and the freight-train wind and the ugly sky. The Coast Guard wasn't here for us. No one was here — not off our port side, not off our starboard.

To stand there with the deck dropping out from under my feet and the water pouring down and seeing nothing! The blood rushed from my head, and my legs buckled. I was dizzy with the sickening truth. *Trashman* was sinking and we were alone. And then it all became a terrifying slow-motion dream.

I saw Mark dive for the compartment at the stern where the life raft filled with emergency supplies was stowed in a fiberglass canister the size of a giant suitcase. I saw Brad on top of the cabin, waves breaking over him, struggling to untie the rubber Zodiac, which was still lashed to the deck. I saw the muscles in his arms as he dug into the iron-hard knots — knots that were being pulled tighter by the force of the sinking boat. I heard the Zodiac burst free, and I saw Brad swimming after it. He pounced on it as it stalled in the leeward shoulder of a wave.

A dark tower of water hanging above the deck came crashing down on Meg and me, dragging us into the rigging of the mainmast. I was under water and then I was up, and I could hear Meg screaming before we were both sucked back toward the stern by another surge.

In the lull between waves I managed to swim away. Treading water and riding the enormous swells, I could see Mark with his arms wrapped around the life raft canister and Meg being lifted forward by another wave. She screamed again as she slammed into the rigging. When she washed back across the deck I saw blood on her arms. The sweatpants she had been wearing were floating free.

"Meg!" I shouted. "Swim away from the boat."

"I can't!"

"Swim away. Wait for a wave to come, then swim away."

I watched her get dragged back into the shrouds. I knew she didn't understand. She didn't know enough about waves to time them so she could get away. I swam back to the boat to try to help her. When I got close, she lunged at me.

I screamed and tried to pry her hands off my shoulders. "Damn it, Meg, you're going to drown us both!" Somehow I pulled her away from the rigging and we were both in the water, free of the boat. I saw Brad holding onto the Zodiac, and I began swimming madly for it.

I grabbed onto the side of the pitching, overturned rubber dinghy, and then Meg was there, then John appeared next to Brad. The four of us clung to the line threaded around the gunwale, stunned by the sight of the sinking boat and Mark, still at the stern, fighting with the life raft canister. It looked as if it was going to pull him under.

Then, in one instant, the canister exploded and the life raft filled with air. The wind caught the raft, and Mark held on, dragged behind it like a fallen waterskier who could not let go of the towline. I held my breath and watched him fight for the raft. If he gets into that boat we'll never see him again, I thought. He won't come back for us. A tremendous gust ripped the raft from Mark's grasp. It blew through the rigging, skimmed the top of a wave, and vanished. Mark swam hard for the Zodiac.

"I couldn't hold it!" he sputtered when he pulled himself up next to Brad. "I couldn't hold it."

Brad ducked under the Zodiac. I shouted for him but got no answer. I tried again — nothing. Come on, Brad, I can't lose you. I can't be out here without you.

"Brad!"

No answer.

"Brad!"

"I'm over here," he finally said. "I'm okay."

"Come back to this side!" I shouted. I wanted him where I could see him.

"No. I'm going to stay over here."

We had drifted fifty feet from *Trashman*. She was heeled over so far that her masts were almost lying on the water. Half the deck was submerged. A wave knocked her upwind, another one slammed into her hull, and she somehow managed to right herself. Her masts shot straight up into the air as if she were making one final stab at survival.

"We're all going to fuckin' die!" Mark shouted. "We're all going to fuckin' die!"

"It's all over, it's all over," John repeated as if he were in a trance.

We dropped into a trough, then rose to the summit of another wave. Now we could see just the tips of *Trashman*'s two masts as they went under. Finally, all that was left of her was the top of the mainmast. I watched in horror as that last bit vanished. The sinking had taken no more than two minutes. And now there was only the raging sea.

"We're all going to fuckin' die!" Mark screamed.

"Shut up, Mark," I shouted back. "Shut up."

I hung on. That was all I could do. Hang on while the dinghy rode the insane contours of the sea. Every wave threatened to yank me away from it. My palms burned. My God, my hands are on fire! I can't hold it. I can't hold it! We slid down into a trough, into a momentary calm.

Am I really here? Am I really here? I thought. I felt so small, so helpless, so exposed — and it had all happened in a heartbeat. Brad had dragged me from my bunk, and then what? Had the life raft really blown away? Had I really just watched *Trashman* be swallowed up by the sea?

I could still hear Mark screaming, but his voice seemed muffled and far off — as if his head was underwater and the words were bubbling up from below. Beneath the steady high roar of the wind I was conscious of the rapid-fire slamming of my heart against my chest. I pressed my forehead against the Zodiac as it climbed another moving hill. I could smell rubber and taste salt on my lips. I became keenly aware of the warmth of the water. Is the water supposed to feel this warm? Or is this what dying feels like?

I looked up again, and though I could still see Mark and John and Meg, they seemed featureless and vague, as though I was viewing them through fogged glass. An enormous wave dragged us up into the sky, and water hit me in the face, filling my mouth and nose. The salt stung my throat. I couldn't breathe. This is it, I thought. This is the end. I felt I was being drawn up into the furious, beating wings of some giant prehistoric bird, and I was powerless, limp, invisible. I was dead. No, I was still alive — but alive in the middle of the ocean with nothing to hold onto but an eleven-foot-long inflatable rubber boat — my God, my God, a boat of air!

Another wave broke over the dinghy, and I fought to keep my grip. I could see the others struggling in the turbulence. When we dropped into the quiet canyon between waves, I screamed again for Brad.

"Talk to me, Brad!" I hollered.

"What!"

I worked my way, hand over hand, to the other side of the dinghy to be next to him.

"What happened?" I asked.

"We fell," he said. He wouldn't look at me. "We fell off a wave. I saw it happen. We fell off and we landed on our side and the water came crashing through the windows. I saw it happen."

I felt the gathering power of another wave, and the Zodiac started climbing again. Then there was an explosion of water, and the dinghy was torn out of my hands. I slammed backward into the water. When I was at last able to surface I could see the Zodiac stalled against the wall of the next huge swell. I stroked as hard as I could, but as I got close, the dinghy was picked up again and flung another twenty feet away. I didn't see any of the others. I screamed for Brad and got a mouthful of seawater. Fighting panic, coughing, praying, I swam again. The muscles in my arms and thighs started to cramp. I lunged for the dinghy and caught the line with the tips of my fingers. As another wave tried to peel me off, I closed my hand around the line and the Zodiac carried me with it on its wild ride. I screamed again for Brad, then for Meg and John and Mark.

I heard Meg calling my name. She was swimming for the dinghy. Then John, Mark, and Brad came up and grabbed onto the side. We had all made it.

"Let's turn it over," Mark said, straining to be heard. "We've got to get in."

Brad and I lifted the windward side while the other three held the line and let the wind carry the Zodiac over. It slapped down onto the water with a ringing thud. We helped Meg climb in. Her legs looked as if they had been slashed by a razor-clawed tiger. Startled, Brad looked at me — I mouthed, "The rigging." The rest of us scrambled aboard. The air was much colder than the water, and I started to shake violently.

We rose up and then, just as we crested, the Zodiac flipped and again I was tumbling, being held underwater, fighting for air. When I surfaced, my head hit the floor of the dinghy and I went down and came up, hitting the floor again. I was trapped! I clawed at the rubber, my lungs tightening. Then I felt the surging sea building under me and I was carried up and thrown forward. When I surfaced, my head was free.

Meg shouted my name, and I turned and saw the dinghy. I swam over and grabbed the line, then closed my eyes and prayed as I had never prayed before. We were on the wind-lashed summits and then we were in the still canyons. I would be torn from the dinghy and then swimming again, swimming for my life, swimming and praying, until I found the hard rubber and reached up and closed my hand around the lifeline.

Minutes went by, maybe five, maybe forty-five. I was trembling uncontrollably. I wanted to stop — I wanted everything to stop. I could feel the heat being drawn from my body and the strength being drained from my legs.

"I'm so fucking cold," Mark said through chattering teeth when the dinghy settled into a trough.

"Me, too," Meg whispered.

"We have to get warm somehow. We can't stay like this," I said.

"We're better off in the water," Brad said.

"Yeah, the air's cold as shit," Mark said. "We have to stay in the water."

"The dinghy won't stay upright anyway," Brad said as we were carried back up into the tumult. When the Zodiac dropped back down, John said, "I want to turn the dinghy over. I want to get in."

"I'm not getting in the dinghy," Mark said.

"It's too cold, John," Brad said. "And we can't keep it upright."

"I want to get in," John insisted.

When I was fifteen, my mother had sent me to a girls' boarding school in Colorado that taught Outward Bound survival skills. Why hadn't I paid more attention? What the hell had they said about hypothermia? I knew one thing; the wind was our biggest enemy right now — whatever body heat we had would be stolen by the wind. We had to shelter ourselves somehow.

"Maybe we could go under the dinghy," I said, thinking out loud.

"You mean hang on under there?" Brad said.

"I don't know. Maybe," I said.

"We'd be out of the wind," Brad said.

"Under?" Meg asked.

"We have to try something," I said as we rose to the

top of a wave and the wind blasted us once more. When we were able to talk, Brad said he thought we should try getting under the boat. Everyone agreed to try it. Brad went under, then resurfaced and said, "I think it will work. Come on."

We all ducked down and came up under the Zodiac. I grabbed the line and treaded water to keep myself up. The odd reddish light made our strained faces look like ghoulish masks. I could just make out the features of the rubber boat: the aluminum floorboards, a black rubber spray cover stretched across the bow, a wire meant to secure the motor when it was being used. I could hear the water slapping against the boat; it was strange — the waves sounded no bigger than those left in the wake of a speedboat. It was deceptively peaceful under there, like being in the clear eye of a hurricane.

"What do you think?" I said to Brad.

"At least we're out of the wind."

"Where's Meg gone off to?" Mark asked.

"She went out. She's claustrophobic," John said.

"We have to get her back in," Brad said.

Brad and John ducked back out of the overturned dinghy, leaving Mark and me alone. We glared at each other. God help me, but I hated him. I hated him for letting the life raft go, for being so weak. I hated him for walking down the dock that day in Annapolis, for walking into my life. At that moment I could have dug his eyes out with my fingernails. I looked away. In a few seconds Brad and John popped back in without Meg.

"Debbie, try talking to her," John said. "She won't come in."

I ducked out. Meg was hanging from the side, her long dark hair pasted to her face, her teeth chattering loudly.

"You ought to get under, Meg," I said. "It will be better."

"No way."

"But it will be warmer, and we'll be together. We have to keep an eye on each other."

"I can't breathe under there. I'm just going to stay out here," she said.

"She won't come," I said when I resurfaced inside. "She says she can't breathe under here."

The four of us hung on in silence and rode the undulating sea. The waves slapped at the rubber.

"Do you think anyone heard the mayday?" Brad said.

"I doubt it," John replied.

"But the Coast Guard knew we were in trouble," Brad persisted. "When they realize we missed the one o'clock and two o'clock calls they'll know something went wrong. Don't you think? I mean, we had that schedule set up and . . ."

"I'm sure they're on the way," I said, buoyed by the image of a gleaming white Coast Guard cutter powering straight for us.

"What do you figure, a couple hours from Charleston?" Brad said.

"Couple, maybe three or four in these seas," John said.

"So that would get them here at what, about five?" Brad guessed.

I asked Mark what time it was now. He was the only one wearing a watch.

"What difference does it make?" he said.

"I want to know, that's all. Just tell me."

"No. It's my fucking watch, and I don't have to tell you anything —"

"Why do you always have to be such a prick?"

"Fuck you," Mark spat back.

"She just asked you what time it is," John said.

"I just don't feel like answering every bloody question she asks me, all right? What time is it, what time is it — who gives a shit what fucking time it is?"

"Anyway, in a little while the Coast Guard will be here, so it doesn't really matter," Brad said.

"Yeah, a couple of hours at most," John said. "They'll be here."

I wanted to believe that. More than anything I wanted to believe it. I was so scared and so cold. My legs were cramped from treading water, and I knew that the more energy I used, the more heat I would lose. I let my legs dangle and tried to hang onto the line using just my arms. But soon my arms got tired and I had to kick again.

"You think they'll have any problem finding us in these seas?" Brad said.

"No," John said. "They're good. They've been in this shit a million times."

"And they know right where we are."

"Yeah."

94

"So we just have to wait," Brad said.

"Jesus, it's cold," Mark said.

"No shit," Brad said.

I hung on and concentrated on breathing, but the more I focused on taking in air the more I felt I wasn't getting enough.

"I don't think there's any oxygen left in here," I said. "You feel it?"

"Yeah," Brad agreed.

"We have to let some air in," I said.

I pushed up on the windward side, and in an instant the Zodiac had flown into the air and landed thirty feet away. I swam as hard as I could to get to it before another wave could fling it farther. One by one we all got back to the dinghy.

"You yabboes!" Mark shouted. "You can't lift it into the fucking wind!"

"Lift it from the leeward side," Brad said.

"And say when you're going to do something before you do it, for God's sake," John said through his clicking teeth.

Everyone, including Meg, ducked back under the dinghy. I treaded water and shivered and tried to remember how long it took for hypothermia to set in. I knew that you would think you were okay, but then you would start losing it and not even know you were in trouble. I also knew you could die if your body temperature sank low enough, even in water this warm. I knew how cold I felt already. If we didn't figure out a way to maintain our body heat, the Coast Guard would find only bodies.

"We've got to get warm somehow," I said.

"Got any suggestions?" Mark said.

"There's not much to work with," Brad said.

"If we could get our bodies closer together. It's the only way to stay warm. We'll freeze to death like this."

We were all quiet again. I tried to think of something to do.

"Oh, my God, what's that?" Brad said. "Did somebody take a shit? Who took a shit under here?"

No one said anything.

"I can't handle that," Brad said. "No way, man, that is disgusting. Who did it?"

"What do you want me to do?" Meg said.

"You did it?"

"I couldn't help it."

"God, that is so foul. I can't believe this," Brad raved.

Meg started to cry, then ducked out from under the dinghy.

"You didn't have to rag on her," John said.

"I just can't handle that."

"She feels bad enough," John said.

"Nobody shit under here. If you have to do it, go outside," Brad said. We were all silent. I felt bad for Meg. But my main concern was how cold I was and how we were going to survive for the next few hours.

"We have to keep thinking of how to get warm," I said. "That's the only important thing right now." After a few seconds I added, "Maybe we could sort of suspend ourselves."

"How?" John said.

"There's that wire there," Brad said, picking up on my idea.

"Yeah?"

"If we could run it across the dinghy and attach it somehow, we could rest our legs on it. Then John and I could hold on here," Brad said, taking the line in one hand, "and we could lay our heads back here . . ." He lay back and rested his head on the rubber spray cover that was stretched across the bow.

"And we could get on top of you," I said. "We'd be out of the water."

"Yeah," Brad said.

"And we'd have our bodies together."

"Let's try it," John said.

John and Brad stretched the wire across the stern and clipped its free end onto the line. Then they got into the position Brad had described. By reaching under each other's backs and grabbing the line on the other side, they were able to lift themselves out of the water. Only their backs and the backs of their legs were still wet.

"Try to crawl on top of us, Deb," Brad said. I pulled myself up and lay across Brad and John. There was enough room for me to fit between them and the floor of the dinghy. And I was out of the water.

"It works," I said. "There's room for more people, too."

"Mark, see if you can crawl on top of me," John said.

Mark scrambled onto the human sandwich we had created. Already I could feel new warmth. And for the first time since we had sunk I was able to rest. We hollered for Meg to come back in. John called to her again, telling her we had found a way to keep warm.

She finally came in.

"Climb on top," John said. "You'll get warm."

"I can't," Meg said. "You know I can't."

"Just try," John said quietly. Meg hoisted her upper body out of the water and lay across Mark and me. Her legs were still hanging in the water.

"I can't do it," she said, sliding down. I didn't know if it was the pain of her deep cuts or her injured back or just the agony of squeezing herself into that tiny space, but I could tell by the sound of her voice that she couldn't be persuaded to do it. She disappeared under the side of the dinghy.

Our system worked well for a while, but then the air got thick again and we knew we had to replenish our oxygen. We got back into the water, lifted the dinghy, let it drop, and climbed back into formation. To keep our air supply fresh, we had to do this every twenty minutes or so. Eventually Brad and John said they were too tired to support Mark and me anymore. I tried taking a turn at the bottom of the pile, but I wasn't quite tall enough to do it. The only way I could hold myself out of the water was to grip the wire with my toes. And with the weight of the others on me I could feel the rough wire sawing into my flesh. I didn't last long.

Each time we lifted the dinghy, we saw a little less light

in the sky. Finally it was totally dark. When night overtook us, the fear and loneliness escalated. We knew it would be almost impossible for the rescue ships to find us in the dark.

Instead of concentrating on making it through the next few minutes, I had to think about living to see the sun come up again. Only with dawn could we hope that a ship would spot us. Maybe they'd send a plane again, maybe the same plane that had checked on us, when, this morning? or yesterday? — I didn't know anymore. All that mattered was that I was in this cold, dark hell with no chance of getting out until dawn. If we could hold it together, if we could keep from going crazy, if Mark could just be quiet, if Meg would just come back under here and do what we told her to do . . .

Poor Meg. Brad, John, Mark, and I had seen the wrath of the ocean before; we knew what it was capable of and we had chosen to come out in it. But Meg didn't have a clue. To her, sailing had been dockside parties, a way to get a tan, have some laughs. She never should have come out here, and John damn well knew it. I could hear the guilt in his voice when he talked to her. He had to deal with that guilt and with the fact that this was ultimately his failure. He would never get another boat to sail; nobody would turn over the helm of their vessel to a skipper who had sunk.

Meg was shouting something — something about a ship. We all ducked out from under the Zodiac. When I surfaced in the darkness, she was saying, "Over there, over there. There's a light!"

When the dinghy rose to the top of a wave, we could see a white light rising and falling with the sea.

"Do you think it's the Coast Guard?" Brad said.

"It looks like a spotlight," I said, straining to keep sight of it as we sank down into a trough.

"Where is it?" Meg asked.

"There," John said. "I see it over there."

"Yes!" I shouted.

Was it the Coast Guard? Or the *Exxon Huntington* or the *Gypsum King*? A fishing boat riding out the storm? It didn't matter — it was a boat.

"They're looking for us!" Brad said.

"Well, they're not going to see us," Mark snarled.

"They'll see us," Meg said weakly.

Again we slid down into a black canyon.

"Damn it," John said.

"Wait," Brad said.

When we rose, the light was there again. The others cheered, but my momentary euphoria was already going cold. The reality of our situation came back into focus. If it was a Coast Guard ship, it was probably using a grid system to search for us. In the darkness they would pass right by us — they might even run us over. And once they had gone by, they would probably eliminate this area from their search territory.

We watched in silence as the light appeared, then disappeared, with each roll of the sea. It grew fainter and fainter, and finally it was gone. With it went our brief joy. The night seemed blacker, the air colder, the sea fiercer.

Four of us went back under the dinghy. Meg stayed outside.

"Let's get back into the pyramid," I said.

"Fuck that," John said. I could hear the defeat in his voice.

"We have to, John, it's the only way we'll stay warm," I said.

"Stay warm? Who's staying warm? I'm freezing my bloody ass off," Mark said.

"We have to do it," I said. "Brad, tell John we have to do it."

"Leave him alone," Mark barked at me. "If he doesn't want to do it, he doesn't want to do it."

Brad, Mark, and I got back into the formation. With only three bodies it wasn't as warm as it had been with four.

"I am so fuckin' cold," Mark said.

"We all are," I said.

"Quit talking about it," Brad said.

"What do you want me to talk about?" Mark retorted.

"Why don't you just shut up." I was so sick of him.

"Don't kick me," Mark said.

"I'm not kicking you."

"You are."

"Mark, I am not doing anything to you."

We went on like that for minutes, which turned to hours. I was so tired. I wanted to sleep, but I was afraid that if I allowed myself to doze off I would never wake up again. We fell into long periods of awful silence, then someone would say, "They'll find us" or "The Coast Guard is good" or "Couple more hours, max," and I would feel a little better. We talked about what we would do as soon as we got home. And we went over and over our recollections of what had happened right before *Trashman* sank. Then we would fall silent again, and the only sounds would be the jackhammer chattering of our teeth and the hollow slapping of the water against the hard rubber. We formed and re-formed the pyramid, sometimes with John, sometimes without him. I found it increasingly difficult to pull myself up out of the water.

Sleep was a siren song; it pulled at me, promising relief. But I couldn't allow myself its comfort. I held on. We all held on. At some point during the night, John went out to check on Meg. When he came back he said he was having pains.

"It feels tight right here." He pressed his palm to his chest.

"Get up here with us," Mark said. "You'll feel better."

I got off Brad and let John climb up. Then I decided to go see Meg.

The first gray wisps of dawn were feathering the sky. The wind seemed to have subsided some, but the seas were still huge and erratic. Waves were coming from every direction.

"It's going to be light soon," I said to her.

"Will that make any difference?"

"Sure. They'll be able to see us," I said.

"You think they're coming?"

"Absolutely."

Brad's head broke the surface. "I think John's having a heart attack."

"Oh, my God," Meg said.

"He's probably just hyperventilating," I said. "Get him out here — he needs air."

"He's got a heart condition," Meg said. "My God, he's going to die."

"He's not going to die, Meg. He just needs air."

"Come talk to him," Brad said.

I ducked under. Meg and Brad followed. John was hanging onto the polypropylene line with one hand. His face was contorted.

"Where does it hurt, John?" I asked.

"I want to turn the boat over and get in," he said slowly. "I can't tread water anymore. It hurts too much."

"But, John —"

"Look, the man wants to get in the dinghy and he's the skipper, so let's get in the dinghy," Mark said.

Meg was in tears. "We've got to do something. He can't die."

"He's not going to die, Meg," Mark said. "You'll be fine, John. We'll turn the boat over and you'll get in and you'll feel a lot better."

"What do you think, Brad? Do you think we can keep it upright?" I said.

Brad shrugged.

"Yeah, come on. John wants to do it," Mark said.

"It's still so rough," I said. "I don't know if we can."

"We're going to do it," Mark said.

Brad and I said we'd try it. We all helped flip the Zodiac, and Brad climbed in first. Then Mark, Meg, and I lifted John up, while Brad pulled. Eventually we got him onto the floor. Then Mark and I boosted Meg on board, while Brad balanced the boat. We all grimaced when we saw her legs. Her gaping wounds were puffy and inflamed.

Mark boosted himself into the dinghy, leaving me alone in the water. I was reluctant to climb in — the air was so much colder than the ocean. And I felt as if I had somehow become a part of the sea. It felt safe, almost amniotic. I let my legs go limp and allowed my thoughts to drift. Maybe the sun would break through the low clouds this morning . . . maybe we would feel its warmth on our puckered skin . . . maybe the sea would quiet and the Coast Guard would see us . . . maybe by tonight I'd be in a warm bed . . . after a hot shower . . .

"It's cold as shit out here," Mark said. "Let's turn it back over."

His words were drowned out by the roar of a tremendous wave overtaking the dinghy. I shouted, and Brad jumped to the windward side as it broke over us. I gripped the line and was still hanging on when the dinghy was released from the force of the wave. It had filled with water but, amazingly, it was still upright. Brad had used his strength and bulk to keep the boat from flipping over.

"Come on, let's turn it back over," Mark said. "It was better that way. We'll freeze to death out here."

"Look, man, if you like it better in the water, then help yourself," John said. "There's a whole ocean out there."

Mark jumped into the water and held on to the dinghy directly across from me. I was getting ready to climb aboard, preparing myself for the shock of cold that I knew was coming.

"Don't kick me," Mark said.

"I'm not touching you," I said.

"You did it again," Mark said. "Cut it out."

"What are you talking about? I'm not kicking you."

"Cut it out."

I popped my head underwater to see where his feet were. I didn't think I had been kicking him, but the last thing I wanted to do was make him more agitated. I was afraid of what he might do.

I opened my eyes and felt the sting of salt water. I waited for my vision to clear. When it did, my stomach contracted. A cold sword of fear stabbed through me. I didn't believe what I was seeing. I didn't want to believe it. Now I knew what had been bumping Mark's legs. Sharks. There were sharks everywhere. Dozens, no, hundreds of them — as far as I could see. Some were so close I could see the membrane hooding their lifeless, clouded eyes. Others were just slow-moving angular shadows spiraling into the depths.

I yelled, "Sharks," and launched myself into the dinghy, landing on top of John. A half-second later, Mark landed on top of me.

"Jesus fucking Christ," he was screaming. "There are sharks everywhere!"

6

Fins broke the water all around us. For every shark that dove, two more seemed to surface. I couldn't believe I had just been in that water, spent maybe eighteen hours in that water with my legs hanging down and with Meg's open cuts . . . If the sharks had been there all along, why hadn't they attacked? And if they hadn't been there, why had they suddenly appeared — and in such huge numbers? What drew them to us now?

We watched them circle while the Zodiac shuddered with the motion of our trembling bodies. A wave picked us up, and we listed precariously to one side before righting ourselves. It was vital that we keep the dinghy balanced. The idea of turning turtle was unbearable.

"We have to find a way to stabilize this thing," I said.

"If we had some kind of sea anchor . . ." Brad said. But what did we have to use? Five bodies and the clothes on our backs and an open boat.

"What if we could get one of these floorboards out . . ." I studied the three aluminum boards that covered the bottom of the dinghy. There was also a small wooden board in the bow covering a storage space. I reached into the bow and was able to pop the wooden board right out.

"All right!" Brad said.

Brad and I talked it over. If we could run the wire through the hole in the board and drag it behind us, maybe it would make the dinghy more stable — and keep us closer to the area where the Coast Guard expected to find us. Brad rigged the wire to the board and tossed it over the side. I waited for the next wave to come, eager to see how it worked. And then, wham! — the dinghy was yanked backward and we all went sprawling. We saw the dorsal fin of a big shark streaking away from us, dragging the Zodiac with it. The shark had gone after the board like a bluefish striking a lure. Before I could scream, the dinghy had stalled as the fin kept moving, and I knew he had spat the board out and swum away.

We all lunged for the line at the same time, almost flipping the dinghy in our panic. Mark got hold of the wire and pulled it in. The big shark surfaced again just off our port side, rising from the blue-black depths like an enemy sub. He was a monster, longer than the Zodiac.

"Get out of here, you fucker!" Mark shouted, raising the board over his head like a sledgehammer and bringing it down on the shark's back.

"Stop!" Meg and I both screamed.

"Are you crazy?" Brad said as he ripped the board from Mark's hands.

"You idiot!" I said.

"Leave it alone," John said.

"If we leave them alone, maybe they'll leave us alone. Like bees, you know?"

Oh sure, Meg, just like bees, I wanted to say. Bees and sharks. God, we were losing it. I looked from one blue-lipped, pale, drawn face to the next. I was sure I looked as bad as they did. I closed my eyes, trying to get away from their death masks, from the sharks, from everything.

I knew a few sailors who had had to be rescued at sea. But somehow I had never imagined myself in that position. Bad things happened to other people — people who didn't know what they were doing, people who were unlucky. The boats I had been on in the past had seemed charmed somehow. I had always felt that no matter what happened, no matter how dicey things got, I would make it through.

But not this boat. I played back the chain of events in my mind. From the moment John and I left Southwest Harbor I had had misgivings. Why hadn't I just listened to my instincts? There were plenty of signs of trouble — Meg showing up and the unreliable engine and the whole thing with Mark. But I had, I had tried to get off! My God, if only I had stood my ground with Newberger. I could have just packed up and walked away. And now here we were — our legs entangled, our lives entangled ... Brad and I at the bow, John and Meg in the stern, Mark in the middle, in a heaving rubber boat.

"Rub-a-dub dub, five men in a tub," I said out loud.

"What did you say?" Brad asked, looking at me as if I had lost my mind. I dipped my hand in the water and felt its warmth. If I could just climb back in for a minute and feel that warmth again. Then I remembered the sharks, and jerked my hand back to my lap.

"Brad — how fast do you think sharks attack?" I asked.

"Why?"

"I was just thinking how nice it would be if I could get back in the water just long enough to warm up, like two seconds."

"You've got to be kidding," Brad said.

"I'm serious."

"Let her go," Mark said. "More room for the rest of us."

"Are you okay?" The way Brad said that frightened me. Maybe the cold was already digging its gnarled fingers into my brain.

"I'm so cold," Meg said and wrapped her arms around her knees.

A gray bird was overhead, riding the stiff air currents. He dipped a wing and wheeled, then dove straight for us, lighting on one of the Zodiac's pontoons right next to Meg. It startled all of us.

"Jesus!" Mark said.

The bird stared at us, and we stared at it. That's food, I thought, but before I could begin to think of a way to catch it, the bird cocked its head, shifted its knobby, webbed feet, and lunged at Meg, striking her in the face with its beak.

"Oh, my God," Meg cried and brought both arms across her head while John shooed the bird away.

"Are you all right?" I asked.

"Is it bleeding?" Meg asked, pulling her hand away from her cheek.

"No," John said.

"Fuckin' bird," Mark said. "I don't believe that."

"He thought we were something to eat," Brad said.

If we don't find a way to get warm, I thought, we *will* be just something to eat. We need to cover ourselves, to seal in what's left of our body heat. Maybe . . . maybe if we put some water in the dinghy, our bodies would warm it up.

"What are we supposed to scoop it up with?" Mark asked when I made my suggestion.

"We could just use our hands," I said.

"Right," Mark said sarcastically.

"It's worth a try. John, don't you think it is?" Meg said.

We all tried splashing water into the boat, but after a frenzied few minutes I knew it was futile. All we had done was lure a dozen more sharks closer to the Zodiac. One rubbed up against the dinghy, and I could feel the vibration of his rough skin against the rubber.

Brad had another idea. He thought there might be a way to open the drainage valve and let water into the boat.

"I thought that only worked to let water out," I said.

"I know, but there has to be a way to rig it to stay open for a few minutes," Brad said.

"And what if we can't get it closed?" Mark said.

Brad didn't reply. He scrambled over everyone's legs and started working on the plug. He couldn't get it to turn. John gave it a try, then Brad tried again. His face reddened as he put all his strength into it.

"Son of a bitch!" Brad said and fell backward. "The damn thing snapped right off." Now we couldn't even open the valve.

"Maybe we can pry the aluminum boards up and use them for shelter," I said. "Maybe we could even use them to signal."

We all agreed that every inflatable we had ever seen had an air-filled bladder that ran down the center of the boat to form a keel, and that it probably kept the floorboards in place, too. Now that we had removed the wooden board from the bow, that end of the bladder was exposed.

"So if we deflate the bladder we ought to be able to get the boards out," I said and the others nodded. But what could we use to puncture the rubber bladder? We had nothing sharp — except our teeth. Brad and I began taking turns chewing at the rubber, gnawing at it like dogs. It was hard and taut, and I found it almost impossible to get even the smallest pinch between my teeth. It was difficult to control their chattering, but I found that if I bit down hard enough I could work the rubber back and forth. Little by little, Brad and I made a divot in the bladder and finally broke through, but only a tiny amount of air hissed from the minute hole. By then we had realized that the floorboards were held tight by the sides of the Zodiac, not just the bladder, and they were not going to budge as long as we were still floating.

"The life raft!" Mark said and pointed ahead of the Zodiac. I saw nothing but waves and sky.

"Where?"

"Paddle!"

"Where?"

"Paddle!" Mark repeated.

"Yeah, I think I see it," John said, sitting forward, then leaning over the side and stroking madly with one arm.

"I don't," Brad said.

"It's over there," Mark said.

I wanted desperately to believe him. I scanned the uneven horizon as we rode the swells. We paddled after the phantom raft for ten minutes or so, never getting another glimpse of it, never getting anywhere at all. Brad and I quit. Mark and John continued paddling for a few more minutes, still convinced they had seen something. The effort had wiped me out, and I sank back against the bow and started to cry. So much energy expended and so little to show for it. I let despair wash over me. We would never live to see the Coast Guard. They might find our raft tomorrow or the next day. But we'd all be dead.

I stared into the water. Something was floating just off the bow. It drifted closer, and I saw that it was a clump of sargasso weed; we were indeed in the Gulf Stream. And then I thought I saw a way for us to get some warmth.

"Seaweed!" I shouted. "We'll cover ourselves with seaweed!" As I lunged to grab a handful, a couple of small dorsal fins broke the water twenty yards away.

"And get our arms chewed off gathering it," John said.

"Not if someone fends off the sharks while I pull it in," I said.

"I don't want that slimy shit on me," Mark said.

"Fine. Freeze to death," I said.

"Don't you two ever stop?" Meg said. "I can't take this anymore."

Brad said he would help. He got ready to beat off the sharks while I reached into the water. I grabbed a mass of weed and felt a surge of pride and optimism as I pulled it in. This might actually work. I paddled a little to bring us to the next patch of weed, then reached in and grabbed it. With every clump of sargasso came all kinds of debris — pieces of Styrofoam and plastic, even a length of polypropylene line — artifacts of humanity, bleached and battered by the sea. I wondered where this stuff had come from, how far it had traveled. What had become of the people who had sipped coffee from this broken Styrofoam cup or looped the end of this line around a cleat?

Again I asked if Mark and John would help pull in

weed. John reached over the side and got a clump. Mark scowled. "You gather it up. It's your stupid idea."

"Are you at all interested in trying to make it out of here alive or are you going to sit there and bitch," I shouted.

Meg winced.

"Debbie, come on," Brad said. "Leave him alone. He doesn't feel like doing it."

When we had a big pile of the mustard-colored weed in the boat I spread it out on top of my legs and torso and tried to cover my arms. Thick and rubbery, it looked as if it could be decent insulation. Meg, John, and even Mark started covering themselves. Brad stayed up on the side of the dinghy, appearing totally absorbed in trying to keep it balanced. Throwing his head back, he yelled, "Fuck you, God. Fuck you, you fucking bastard!"

"Yeah, fuck you, motherfucker!" Mark joined in.

No! They don't mean it. Don't listen to them, God! I prayed He hadn't heard them or, if He had, that He understood they didn't know what they were saying. If we ever needed God on our side, it was now. I had always believed in God in a vague, Sunday-school way. Now I found myself talking to Him, one to one, and listening for a reply. I had to believe He was up there, beyond the blank sky. He could see us. He had a plan, a reason for putting us through this nightmare. I had to believe that was true.

Is this a test? I asked silently. Is this some sort of wake-up call? I hear it, okay? Just give me a break here. I've screwed some things up, I'll grant you that, but I have to tell you I don't want to die. Whatever bad stuff I've done, I can't believe you would punish me this way.

I pictured my mother getting the phone call and tried to imagine what she would do when she heard the news. She'd probably be devastated — who would she blame for all the shit in her life if I were gone? No, Debbie, that's not fair. Don't think like that. I'm sorry, God. Look, I'm not going to try to bargain with you. But if you get me through this I'll try to do better. I'll try to change. Is that why you are doing this to me? To get me to change my life? I will, I will. I mean I'll try. I don't want to die. But I'm so afraid to make promises I may not be able to keep. I'm just so tired, so tired . . .

✓

Sand in my mouth. I lift my head and open my eyes. Smudged sky, blurred sea. The wind, so cold. Next to me, the body of a woman. The body stirs. Tilly! Tilly, from back in Annapolis!

"Tilly. Wha . . ." My voice is muffled, unfamiliar. Had my lips moved?

"How did you get here?" she says.

"I don't know."

"My boat sank. I couldn't get to the life raft. I must have washed up here. Is that what happened to you?"

"I don't know," I say. "Where are the others? Where's Brad?"

"There's nobody here, Debbie."

"We have to find help. I think they're still out there."

In the distance, gray shingled houses on stilts, boarded

up for the winter. One house sits high on a hill, smoke drifting out of a chimney.

"We'll find someone there." I point.

"We can't climb that hill," Tilly says, crying. "We can't climb —"

We are in front of the house. I cup my hands around my eyes and peer through a sliding glass door. Steaming teacup on a table. Dried hydrangeas in a Japanese vase.

"Come on!" I slam my fists on the glass. "Open up!" A woman approaches. Her face clouds. She brings her hand to her mouth and screams, a high-pitched tea kettle scream.

Tilly and I back away. In the glass we see what she sees. Open sores, raw and weeping, all over our faces, our arms, our legs. No one will come near us now. I hear myself wail . . .

"Debbie, Debbie! Wake up! Come on," Brad was shaking me. The fog lifted, and my teeth began chattering so violently my jaw muscles cramped up. "Are you okay?"

I smelled the dank weed and the foul water in the dinghy and I knew where I was. There was no beach, no Tilly, no house, no steaming cup of tea. I felt something bite my foot, then my shoulder and the backs of my knees.

"Shit, something's chewing on me, " I said. "Like little crabs. Are they getting you, too?"

I grabbed a handful of the sargasso and examined it closely. I was dazzled by the life it supported — all on this rotten little branch of seaweed. There was an entire world, self-sufficient and complete. Tiny crabs and shrimp and mussels and probably a hundred other things too small to see. They were all alive, oblivious to the cold and the wind and the storm-whipped waves. The sight of them cheered me — until I felt the crabs pinching me again.

"Shit," I said again. I wondered if they could break skin — I had an awful vision of them burrowing into my flesh. I picked up a little crab and crushed it between my fingers. I grabbed another and another. Some were too quick for me. I would think I had one, then it would escape and burrow into the weed and start nibbling on me again.

I crushed another one and stuck it in my mouth, but I gagged and spat it out. I wasn't that desperate yet. I watched a crab run across my chest. If I die, how long will it take them to strip the flesh from my bones? I shook my head. Don't picture those things. Stop. I saw a bleached skeleton, picked clean.

"Stop!" I shouted out loud.

"Stop what?" John asked.

I was frightened by the way I seemed to be losing control of my thoughts. This must be the beginning of dying. Or maybe I'm just going nuts. It must be the cold. I felt my mind sliding down, going deeper and deeper into a black and bottomless cavern.

"Brad, I'm scared. I think the cold is getting to me. I think I have hypothermia," I said through chattering teeth.

Brad dropped down next to me.

"They'll be here soon. They know where we are.

Maybe they'll send another plane out to check on us," he said. "It won't be much longer."

"If the sun would just come out," John said. "At least we might be able to figure out what direction we were going."

"When we sank, the wind was blowing out of the northeast, right?" I said. "I don't think it's changed."

"Yeah, but what about the Gulf Stream?" John said. "It runs south to north."

"So we wouldn't have gotten too far," Brad said. "We shouldn't be too far from where the Coast Guard spotted us."

"What's taking them so long?" Meg asked. It was the first time she had spoken in a long time. I was relieved to see that she was mentally still with us. I looked down at her legs. Her wounds looked awful, inflamed and festering.

"How're you doing, Meg?" I asked. "Are you okay?"

Mark shifted his position and bumped Meg's legs, making her cry out in pain.

"Hey, man, watch it," John said to Mark. "You just kicked her."

"I couldn't help it," Mark said. "You have all that room to stretch out. I don't have shit."

"Just be a little more careful next time," Brad said.

"I don't have any bloody room."

We were all quiet again. Brad continued to balance the Zodiac as we rode over the swells. The ocean had settled down since the night before, but I didn't trust the relative calm. A rogue wave could hit us at any time. I offered to take a turn balancing the dinghy, but Brad said he wanted to keep doing it. He seemed to need that focus, and I sensed he wanted to separate himself from all the petty crap going on among those of us sitting on the floor. It was strange — he didn't even seem to be cold.

I remembered that he had been wearing long underwear with his jeans when we were on watch. Had it been that cold when we were on watch? Why didn't I have on long underwear? What the hell was I doing in these stupid little running shorts? I looked at Meg. All she had on was John's flimsy shirt. I felt guilty for wishing for more when she had almost nothing. Then I wondered why Brad hadn't offered to give Meg his underwear. Wasn't that the right thing to do? Maybe I should say something. But if I say something it might start a huge fight. Everybody would want the long johns, and Meg is the one who needs them and she probably couldn't get them on anyway and then Brad would be mad . . .

"Look!" John said. "Over there."

I looked over my shoulder and saw a boat way off in the distance.

"Paddle," Mark yelled, then picked up the wooden floorboard and started power-stroking with it.

We all paddled and hollered, "Here, over here!" When Mark got tired I took the board from him and forced it through the water with all my strength. After a few minutes we could see we were getting nowhere. The ship had gotten smaller; it was heading away from us.

Despair dropped over me like a heavy, wet net.

"A ship would have to be right on top of us to see us," I said.

"And even then they'd have to really be looking," Brad said.

"Didn't anyone tell them we were fucking out here!" Mark's face was flushed with rage. "Does anyone even know that we're out here, for Christ's sake? You just watch. We're all going to die, you know, we're going to . . ."

"Shut up, Mark." I wanted to hit him. "If you don't stop talking like that, we will die."

"Just ignore him," Brad said, touching my arm. "Don't pay any attention to him, don't talk to him." He said it as if Mark weren't there.

Mark muttered something about needing more room and stretched his legs out straight, jostling Meg again.

Dusk descended, and I watched as the light — and the hope — drained away. Somewhere to the west, the sun was still high in the sky, the soil was warm and fragrant. I closed my eyes. There was a ball game in a mowed green field and children on backyard swings and dogs barking and cars turning in to driveways. There was life out there, life on earth. But here, on this bleak little rubber planet, there was only misery and stink and cold. I had never seen such darkness, felt such total desolation.

"They won't see us now, not for the rest of the night," I said.

"No shit." Good old Mark.

"I don't know if I can handle another night," John said.

"Not much choice, bro," Brad said wearily.

Meg was quiet and still as a statue. I wondered if the others were having crazy spells the way I was, drifting in and out of reality. I wondered how close we all were to really losing it, dropping over the edge. I figured we'd been out here for something like thirty hours, more than half of which had been spent in the water — water that was probably thirty degrees warmer than the air, which had to be forty or forty-five degrees. I didn't know how long we could expect to survive in these temperatures. If it got much colder we'd never make it through to morning.

"Thank God we're in the Stream," I said, wanting only to hear my own voice, to make sure I was capable of speaking and making sense. "If we weren't, we wouldn't have the sargasso and we'd be a hell of a lot colder."

Nobody responded; they just stared and shivered. The sound of our chattering teeth filled the moonless night. And the stench of rotting seaweed and pus and urine was overpowering. We had agreed to relieve ourselves over the side — for Meg's sake, we had said. I had done it at first, but then, guiltily, I had gotten lax and discovered the incredible warming effect that urinating produced. I agonized over giving that up to protect Meg, feeling somehow that I had a right to my own body's fluids. I hoped I wasn't hurting Meg, but she had to be urinating in the boat, too, so what difference did it make?

I watched Meg for a while. I couldn't tell if her eyes were open or closed. For a moment I thought she might be dead. Then she groaned and shifted her weight. Survival of the fittest, I said to myself. If that was the case, Meg didn't stand much of a chance out here.

When John and Meg and I had sailed the boat to Annapolis, John had pointed out Montauk on Long Island as we passed it in the night. He said Meg had been born there and we would all go there someday and party. I felt bad that I didn't know more about her. She had mentioned an ex-husband once, and a house in Florida. Other than that, what did I know about this woman who was suffering so a few feet away from me? I knew she liked her chardonnay very cold. I stared at Meg and wondered if she was thinking about home right now, if she was searching the horizon for the hazy white lights of Montauk Point.

A huge wave crashed onto the dinghy, filling it with water. I immediately started bailing with cupped hands. We had let our guard down, forgotten the threat of being flipped. We had to be more careful. The water actually felt good in the boat, but the weight caused the Zodiac to ride lower. If another big wave hit, we could easily be swamped. A little water in the dinghy made it more comfortable — too much made it deadly.

"Look, over there," Meg said, pointing. "I think I see a light."

We all turned, and when we rose to the top of a swell I saw it, too. It was near enough that we could see it was some kind of masthead or anchor light. There didn't seem to be any running lights.

"God, it's close," Brad said.

"Maybe a fishing boat?" I said.

"We could try to paddle over. Take turns paddling with the board from the bow," John said.

"Give it to me," Brad said, reaching for the board.

My heart started to race. If it was a fishing boat, the chances were good that it would stay in that one spot for a while. We might be able to reach it. Brad grunted with effort as he drove the board through the water. The rest of us stroked with our hands. I knew I wasn't doing much good, but it was better than doing nothing.

We reassured each other that we were indeed moving toward the light. Then, as if to give us further encouragement, it began to rain. We stopped paddling, lay back, and opened our mouths, ready for the deluge to begin. But the light rain quickly faded to a sprinkle, then barely a spit. Mother Nature spitting in our faces. That idiotic television commercial ran through my head. It's not nice to fool Mother Nature . . . it's not nice to fool . . . John cursed, then took the board from Brad and paddled with choppy, angry strokes.

I told John we were gaining on the boat, but after about twenty minutes the truth became painfully obvious. The winds and the waves and the current were all working against us — we hadn't made any progress at all. Still, we continued taking turns with the board until dawn broke and we saw that the boat, if that's what it was, had dropped over the horizon and disappeared.

We all were exhausted. But at least we had made it through the night. The new day brought renewed hopes of rescue. Surely the Coast Guard was out in full force by now. Surely this would be the day.

7

The storm had moved on, though the ocean still heaved with pewter-smooth swells. The clouds were milky and higher but still unbroken. The sky wasn't giving up anything — no rain to quell our relentless thirst, no sun to warm our puckered skin, no clue, even, as to what direction we were traveling.

I sensed that a change had come over the crew in the night. Whatever alliances we had formed seemed stronger; boundaries were more clearly defined, more fervently defended. Mark had cut himself off from everyone. Though only an arm's length from me, he acted as if he were in the dinghy alone. His face was white, his lips tinged with blue, his pale eyes fixed on something unseeable out past the rolling waves.

John and Meg huddled together at the stern. John had his arm around Meg and his head resting on hers. Meg's matted hair was pasted around her face like a dark shroud. Her eyes looked sunken and dim. Brad sat stone-faced and silent up on the side of the Zodiac. He had his mission; he was the balancer of the boat.

I sat at the bow and studied my skin, horrified and fascinated by what new ways the sea had found to eat away at me. My legs and arms were pocked with open sores; every little scratch had mushroomed into a raw wound. A deep cut next to my right little toe was inflamed. I had always thought salt water had a healing effect; now it seemed as toxic as acid. When I lay down, every roll of the dinghy sent the rank bottom water rushing toward my mouth; I had to time my breaths to avoid swallowing any. I closed my eyes and started saying the Lord's Prayer, losing myself in the familiar words, feeling strengthened by the simple fact that I could remember them.

I asked God for strength, then ridiculed myself for thinking there was a God. I apologized to God for doubting his existence. My mind seemed trapped in this rapid-fire volley, thoughts rocketing by like snipers' bullets. Control, I said to myself. I must maintain control. Our Father, who art in Heaven.

"There's a ship," Mark said suddenly.

I sat up and saw it. It looked huge, like a container ship or a tanker. I reached over the side and began paddling. Adrenaline rushed through my body with a high-voltage jolt.

"Come on, Brad, paddle!" I shouted, but he only dipped his hand in the water halfheartedly. I stroked hard for a few minutes, knowing deep down that it was futile but still feeling compelled to try, to do something. I don't know how long I pulled before I realized the ship was gone. Everyone else had slumped back into their places.

I fell against the side, exhausted. Brad had gotten down on the floor next to me and was sitting with his knees pulled up to his chin, arms wrapped around his legs. He was suddenly shaking violently.

"I don't know how much longer I can handle this," he said in a quivering voice. "I can't take it. I'm too cold." The boat rocked with Brad's convulsing body. It terrified me seeing him like this.

"Could you guys get on top of me? I think I'm freezing to death," he stammered.

Mark moved toward him, bumping Meg's legs again, making her moan. Brad lay down, and Mark and I draped our bodies over him. He was shaking so fiercely it felt as if we were trying to subdue a madman. Mark and I locked arms and tried to hold Brad tighter, to create a seal of body heat.

"What are they doing to Brad?" Meg cried. "John, stop them! Stop them!" She seemed to think we were attacking him.

John tried to calm her, but she flailed at him, pleading

with him to stop us. She clawed at John until he slapped her across the face and she collapsed in sobs.

In a minute or two Meg was calmer. She seemed to understand now that we were trying to help Brad. And with John's help, she even managed to move over to us. She and John climbed on top of our flattened pyramid. We stayed like that for a long time, until finally Brad's trembling subsided.

We moved back to our corners, again absorbed in our own discomfort. Mark stretched and kicked, trying to create more room for himself. Meg wailed in agony. John rambled on and on about needing water.

"Mark," I heard John say, "if you kick Meg again I'm gonna knock the shit out of you."

I stole a look at Meg's legs. Red streaks were radiating up from one of the deepest cuts. I knew that meant blood poisoning. I bent over and whispered to Brad to look.

"We have to do something," I said.

"Like what?"

"I don't know." I saw the piece of polypropylene line we had found in the seaweed. "Maybe put a tourniquet around her leg just above the cut to keep the infection from spreading. Just to buy some time until the Coast Guard gets here."

"What are you guys talking about?" Meg sounded upset. "You're talking about me, aren't you? I know you are. John, they are talking about me."

"We're worried about your leg," I said. "We think it's infected. Look."

Meg unfolded her arms and looked at her right leg and began to cry.

"I was thinking we should put a tourniquet on it," I continued. "It will keep the infection from spreading. Just till the Coast Guard comes. Understand?"

"That might be a good idea, Meg," John said.

"I don't think I can move my legs," she sobbed.

"We'll help you," he said. His voice had new life, as if the prospect of aiding Meg in some way had energized him.

"Mark, trade places with me," I said and scrambled over him to get to Meg. I tried to make enough room for Meg to spread her legs out straight, but she couldn't do it without hitting John or Mark. John and I helped her up and got her to sit on the side of the dinghy. Tears streamed down her face. I hadn't realized until that moment that Meg was naked except for her shirt. Even her underpants were gone.

No wonder she had stayed huddled with her arms wrapped around her legs. She tried to reach down and cover herself, and my heart ached for her. She was in such pain, yet she was still trying to hold onto a shred of her dignity. I wanted to tell her to forget about the tourniquet. I wanted to tell her that everything was all right, that everything was going to be fine.

"I know this is going to hurt," I said gently, "but you have to stretch out your leg so I can get the rope around it." I felt overwhelming guilt for asking her to further expose herself and for the agony I knew I was about to inflict on her. But I believed that it was absolutely necessary for her survival.

Meg moved her swollen, inflamed leg out toward me, sobbing in pain. John held her steady as I ran the piece of yellow line under her leg about three-quarters of the way up her thigh, then tied an overhand slipknot. I began to pull it tight, and Meg screamed, a tortured, soul-wrenching scream. John grabbed her hands and tried to restrain her, but she fought him. I couldn't do this to her. I released the knot.

"I was only trying to help you, Meg, that's all," I said. She crumpled down to the floor of the dinghy. I felt sick — over the pain I had caused her and the knowledge that we had bungled what was probably our only chance to help her. My heart pounded. I couldn't look at Meg. I couldn't look at any of them.

She is going to die, I said to myself. Oh, God, I didn't mean to hurt her. Please forgive me. What are we going to do if she dies? I feel as if I'm going to vomit. I can't take much more of this.

One dark fin, then another, broke the water a hundred yards away. They were still out there, keeping their vigil. I lowered myself back into my position in the bow. I had been so absorbed in Meg's agony that I had forgotten for a few minutes about the cold. But now my body resumed its shaking with an intensity that scared me. I tried to stop it, tried to focus on something other than the trembling, tried to corral my thoughts — concentrate, concentrate on anything other than the cold.

The Coast Guard. Where the hell was the Coast Guard? They don't just leave people out here, not after you ask for help, not after they see you and know where you are and know you are in trouble. But where were they? It had to be afternoon, and the seas had quieted down. Surely they could navigate this. Anybody could navigate this. Had they abandoned us out here? Left us here to die?

⌁

"I can't take sitting in this shit anymore," I heard Mark say. I had been sleeping. The afternoon light had dimmed. "It's making me sick. We have to get this stinking shit out of here."

"We can't get it out," John said.

"Yeah, we can. We can turn this thing over and wash the crap out."

"What about the sharks?"

"You see a shark right now? I don't see a shark right now," Mark said.

"Just because you don't see them . . ." John said.

"We'll do it quick. Just flip the fucker over and flip it back up."

"How do you think Meg is going to get in and out of the dinghy?" John asked.

"She won't be able to do it," I said. "And we'll lose all the seaweed, and then how are we going to keep warm if we have to spend another night out here?"

"We'll gather more if we have to," Mark replied.

"There isn't any more. We haven't seen any in a long time," Brad said.

"I don't give a fuck. We're turning this bastard over now." Mark started rocking the boat back and forth, banging everyone with his legs. He looked like a five-year-old throwing a temper tantrum.

"Stop it," we all said, but he kept rocking.

"Brad," I said under my breath. "Do something."

"Mark, cool it," Brad said. "We're not going to do it, so just forget about it. We're all too weak. What if we turn it over and we can't get back in — and the sharks come back?"

"The crap in the water is only making Meg worse. Look at my legs, look at yours. We've all got these sores, and they're getting bigger and more infected by the minute. If we get some clean water in here maybe they won't get any worse."

What Mark was saying made sense. He had an irritating ability to be reasonable when he wanted to. And he was right, the bottom water was horrendous, the smell intolerable. The sores on my skin had grown since last night; now they were the size of dimes. And when I looked closely I could see new ones opening up all over my body.

The warmth of the water enticed me. And no sharks were visible at the moment. Maybe we could . . . if we went quick and we didn't splash . . . John said something to Meg and she nodded.

"Meg thinks she'd like to try," John said.

"Don't be an idiot, man. She won't be able to do it," Brad said.

"If we do it fast — lower Meg in first, then we all get in real quietly so we don't draw attention to ourselves," John said. "Then we flip it over, get it back up, and grab all the seaweed and throw it back in. I think it will be okay."

Brad protested, but now he was the lone dissenter. We were going to do it. We gathered all the seaweed into the center of the Zodiac. Then we got Meg up on the side, turned her so that her legs were hanging in the water, and as gently as we could, slid her down into the water. Brad and John got out on the windward side, then Mark and I lowered ourselves over the leeward side. I was at the bow, Mark at the stern. Meg hung on to John while we lifted the windward side of the Zodiac into the air. When it was high enough, Mark and I pulled from our side until it flopped over. I scanned the water for sharks. Nothing out there right now. Feeling little triggerfish nibbling at my legs, I fought the urge to kick them away; we had to be as motionless as possible. The sharks would be attracted by any movement.

The water felt wonderful, but we had no time to savor its soothing warmth. We had to get the Zodiac upright. Once we had it righted, we scrambled back in and landed on top of each other in the bottom of the dinghy. Everyone except Meg.

"Come on, Meg," John said.

"I just want to hang here for a few more minutes," she

said in a dreamy voice. Her eyes were closed. I understood how she must feel. The weightlessness was such a relief, and the warmth was seductive. We all froze, waiting for Meg, waiting for the sharks.

"Shit, the seaweed," Brad said. "Grab what you can before it floats away."

We had been so worried about Meg we had let the weed drift off. Brad and I leaned over and managed to get about half of it back into the dinghy.

"All right, that's it, Meg," I said, ashamed at the obvious anger in my voice. "Get in now. We can't take a chance. Come on."

I reached out for her. She pulled away for a moment, then relented. We all helped haul her back in. She had so little strength left that she couldn't give us much assistance. Although we tried to protect her battered legs and bruised back, she screamed as we dragged her over the side. I told myself we had done the right thing. We were back in the dinghy, all of us, and the fetid water was gone.

"Now there's not enough weed to cover us all," Brad said. "We're going to freeze to death."

I didn't respond. I was just relieved to have gotten rid of the disgusting soup in the dinghy. That relief lasted for about two minutes, until I realized that we had done an incredibly stupid thing. The bottom water had been rank, but it had also been warm. Now we had lost half of our weed and all of our body-heated water.

I fell back against the side. Flipping the boat over had sapped my strength and heightened my already intense thirst. I looked at the dark gray-green water. No, that wasn't the answer. I knew that drinking salt water would be deadly.

I lay down and stuck my head up under the rubber piece that covered the bow. Ducking under there was a way to escape from the others. Even though they were only a few feet away, I felt as if I was in my own world up there, and I desperately needed to separate myself from them if I was going to keep myself together. They were dragging me down, filling my head with black thoughts. I closed my eyes and could feel sleep's heavy blanket enfolding me. Then I was gripped with fear, and my eyes flew open. Suddenly I didn't want to be alone; I couldn't stand another second of this isolation.

"Brad," I said. "I need you."

Brad ducked under the bow cover.

"I'm scared I'm going to fall asleep and I won't wake up."

"I'll watch you," he said.

"Don't let me sleep too long. Hypothermia can just —"

"I know, Debbie," he said wearily.

I closed my eyes, and a swirl of scenes filled the dark screen of my mind. I saw the Coast Guard plane swooping down on us, the vanishing tip of *Trashman*'s mast, my father, my mother, my half-brother. Then I saw the yellow fire of September aspens, snow on a craggy mountain summit, and the stern face of Mr. Pitman, my high school English teacher — the one who had led my wilderness trips, who had taught me about survival. Mr.

Pitman . . . I hadn't thought about him in years. And yet here he was, in a dark-paneled classroom, standing at a lectern, looking at me, waiting for me. Why did the Ancient Mariner shoot the albatross, Miss Scaling? Are you with us, Miss Scaling? The albatross, why the albatross? And why did he have to wear it around his neck? Not an albatross, Mr. Pitman, a plane, I am saying. Hear the plane? They've come back for us.

I opened my eyes. I had been dreaming again about, what, a bird? No, a plane. I *had* heard a plane. I still heard it. I was awake and I could still hear an engine. Yes! They're back! I knew they'd come. I ducked out from under the bow cover, ready to greet our rescuers. Everyone was looking up — but why was no one celebrating? I scanned the gray sky, then I saw it. We all saw it, a huge silver airliner sailing through the clouds. I pictured the passengers, relaxed in their stocking feet, spreading soft butter on a square of rye bread, glancing out the window and seeing nothing, nothing but the vacant, boundless sea. The plane streaked across the sky and vanished.

I crawled back under the bow cover. My spirits had nose-dived. It seemed useless now to even dream about rescue. The Coast Guard had forgotten about us. No ship, no plane was going to stumble upon us. No bird was going to soar down out of the clouds and snatch us up in its safe talons. They aren't coming, I said to myself. No one is coming. Not now, not ever. I had to face facts. We all did. We were on our own.

I felt a sudden, excruciating pain in my injured toe,

shooting up my leg like liquid fire. I cried out and tried to sit up, but my head hit the bow cover. My toe, my toe! — someone was trying to rip it off my foot. I got out from under the rubber cover to find Mark yanking on my little toe, saying, "I told you to just pull it off. It's so infected it's just going to fall off anyway."

"Leave it alone. Don't touch it!" I kicked at him and caught him in the chin. He fell back against the side.

"Did you see that, Brad?" I asked. "The guy tried to rip off my toe."

"Mark, don't rip off Debbie's toe," Brad said without emotion.

"She's going to lose it. I was trying to help."

"Don't touch me again."

"I don't want to touch you."

"Asshole."

"Cunt."

"Cut it out," John said.

"Can you try to just cool it until the Coast Guard gets here?" Brad asked.

I sat back and looked at Brad and Mark and Meg and John. It was all so clear to me. We were idiots, fools — hoping, no, expecting, to be saved. It had been forty-eight hours since we went down. I couldn't believe the others hadn't figured it out yet.

"I got news for you all," I said. "The Coast Guard isn't coming."

The four of them turned and looked at me but said nothing. Meg dropped her forehead on her knees and began to cry. Fine. Let them sit here waiting, I told myself. I knew the truth now. Nobody was going to save us. We had to save ourselves. I looked away. The sight of them made me sick. How many other people had found themselves in this kind of desperation, and how many had lived through it? What separated the survivors from the nonsurvivors?

I had met a man once in St. Thomas, a crusty old salt who wore one earring. He told me that if a sailor wearing a hoop earring ever fell overboard, Neptune would fish him out by the hoop and haul him back on board. And if a sailor wearing a black pearl was ever lost at sea, he could trade it to Poseidon for his life. The old man wore a black pearl on a chain around his neck. I laughed at him. A few weeks later, in a jewelry store with a friend, I noticed a single black pearl on a hoop in the case. Twenty minutes later I walked out of the store with it in my ear.

Now I reached up and touched the earring. I fingered the pearl. Trade it for your life, the old man had said. I knew it was just a story. Poseidon, the Ancient Mariner, they were just made up. They didn't mean anything. I reached up and pulled the earring out of my ear. I looked at it for a minute, then tossed it into the water.

"What was that?" Brad asked.

"Nothing."

Darkness brought with it a more complete despair, a more thorough loneliness. We knew we would be unseeable for twelve hours, and we knew we would have to fight night's piercing cold. I wanted to reach up and pull the light back, slide it back over the roof of the world.

I lay down next to Brad. My stomach growled noisily.

It was strange, but I didn't feel all that hungry. There was just a vague emptiness, a subtle gnawing need for something, anything. Food had always been such agony for me; for as long as I could remember, it had been both punishment and reward. I thought of all the meals I had vomited up — all the guilt, all the humiliation, all the sneaking around. Stupid, Debbie. Very stupid.

I heard Meg whimpering. Brad coughed and opened his eyes.

"What are we gonna do?" I said to Brad.

"I don't know," Brad said.

"I'm so sorry I got you into this. Your sister is going to kill me."

"At least we're together."

"If I didn't have you . . . if it was just me and those guys . . . I don't know. And Meg, man, she's in such pain."

"I know."

"We're going to make it, aren't we?"

"We just have to stick together, you and me."

"I'm so tired," I said.

"Why don't you go to sleep now. I'll watch you. I'll make sure you're okay."

"Thanks."

I felt myself drifting into sleep.

"Deb?"

"Yeah?"

"When this is all over and we're out of here, we'll always be together, won't we?" Brad asked.

I opened my eyes and looked at him. I thought I

knew what he meant, but I wasn't sure I could make that promise. He needed to hear it, though. We needed each other right now. Always, well . . . always was a long way off.

"Yeah, Brad. We'll always be together," I said and closed my eyes to see a bone-white bird, big as the night, swooping down on me.

8

"I need more fucking room!" Somebody was screaming at me and hitting me. I opened my eyes. Mark.

"You're taking up too much room." He kicked me again. "She's dying. I have to get away from her."

I felt the dinghy rocking. I tried to get oriented. It was dark and my teeth were chattering. I couldn't feel my feet at all. Seaweed was tangled around my body, and I had an awful taste in my mouth. Meg was moaning and Mark was yelling at me and I had been sleeping and I couldn't get ahold of where I was or what was happening.

"Brad?" I called, reaching out. He wasn't there. I shouted for him again and pulled myself out from under the bow cover. I tried to focus in the blackness. I could make out John and Meg, huddled together, and Brad, sitting on the starboard side of the dinghy.

"What are you doing?" I asked.

"I'm just giving Mark some more room so he'll be quiet," he said flatly, never taking his eyes off John and Meg. John had his arms around Meg, and the two of them were rocking back and forth. Meg moaned, John rocked. Meg moaned, John rocked. I wanted to look away, but I kept staring.

"I need water," John said. "I need water."

"My ankle's cut," Mark said, clutching his foot. "It's infected. I know it's infected. What if I get the same disease she has? I have to move, I need more bloody room. Look at her, she's gonna die. She's gonna die. I have to get away from her. She's gonna die."

I knew I should try to shut him up, but I said nothing. I didn't have the energy. Maybe Meg couldn't even hear him now. What was the point of trying to stop anyone from doing anything? Mark was screaming and John was rocking and Meg was moaning and Brad was just sitting there staring at nothing. The stench and the filth and the rot and the emptiness — it was the darkest, darkest nightmare.

If only it would rain, I thought. A warm rain, soft and steady. Everything would be better if I could feel the rain on my skin, let it run over me, wash it all away. I started reciting the Twenty-third Psalm — the Lord is my shepherd, I shall not want. I wanted to see if I could remember the words, the simple, soothing words — words that fell like raindrops, leaving soft circles of hope.

Sometime later, everyone was quiet again. Brad was up on the side. Meg, John, and Mark all seemed to be asleep. The dinghy moved from wave to wave, my teeth chattered, the wind blew. Silence is so loud, I thought.

"Brad," I whispered.

"What?" I had startled him.

"Why don't you come down here and get some sleep? Aren't you freezing up there?"

"I'm okay," he said and looked away.

"Please, Brad. I need you down here."

He didn't move. I was so afraid he would fall asleep and then drop off the Zodiac if we hit a wave.

"Please. I'd just feel a lot better if you were down here. It's not very safe sitting up there."

Without a word he lowered himself down next to me. We huddled together and I felt better. I allowed myself the great luxury of sleep.

Meg was moaning again. Mark was whining about not having any room. John was babbling about water. They were driving me insane, the three of them. If Meg would just shut up — my God, how could I be angry at Meg for moaning? How could I be so heartless? I started in on the whys again. Why this? Why now? Why me? I was imperfect. I had done some not-so-great things in my life. But this? This was my punishment? I felt I was supposed to learn something from this ordeal, some key, something magical and pure. And when I found it I would take it . . . Shit, where would I take it now? I dozed off again.

"Debbie," Brad was whispering. It was still dark.

"Yeah?"

"Listen. What do you think they're doing?"

I lifted my head and strained to see the others. I could see two forms — John and Mark — leaning over the stern.

"What are they doing?" Brad said again.

I couldn't hear what they were saying. I felt a rush of panic. Were they doing something to the boat? Or to Meg? No. Meg was all right. She was sitting with her head on her knees, asleep. I could hear the two guys splashing water. Then I understood. They were drinking seawater. I was stunned. How could they be so stupid?

"They're drinking it," I said to Brad. "Should we stop them?"

"It's probably too late," Brad said.

I felt such sadness listening to them. They had given in, they had lost control. I knew that drinking seawater was a terrible mistake — I remembered hearing that you should drink your own urine first. I didn't know what would happen to them. Would they go mad, or had they already? Would they die? Would they try to do something to the rest of us?

"Brad. Promise me you won't drink it," I whispered.

He didn't answer. That scared me even more. I dropped my head back down, and the water in the dinghy sloshed up around my mouth. I imagined myself opening my mouth and drinking; hanging my head over the side and letting the ocean flow in. How would it taste? How would it feel?

Dawn broke, and for the first time since the sinking it looked as if we might see the sun. The clouds were breaking up. The thought of feeling the sun on my skin gave me a renewed sense of hope. Maybe the Coast Guard was coming after all. Of course they were. So they had some problems getting to us, okay. But now the sea was calmer and there was no reason they couldn't get to us today — hell, maybe they'd be here within the hour.

Don't be a fool, Debbie. If the Coast Guard was looking for us they would have found us by now. They aren't coming; that's all there is to it. "God helps those who helps themselves," my grandmother Queenie used to say. I will help myself, I thought. All I have is myself. I will not fall apart.

Brad ducked out from under the bow. Mark and John stirred, and Meg groaned. Her bad leg looked even worse; the gruesome red streaks had become wider, and now they ran all the way up, disappearing under her shirt.

"They'll come today," John said.

"They better. Look at my ankle," Mark said. The infection in his ankle had spread down to his foot. "What am I going to do?"

"The sun is over there," Brad said slowly, "so it seems like the wind is northerly and the seas are from the northeast. We should be drifting toward land. We might just wash ashore sometime in the next couple of days."

"South Carolina or Georgia, maybe," Mark said.

I was cheered by that image, washing up on a low barrier beach.

"What do we do when we get there?" Meg asked. "Go to the Coast Guard station?"

"Hell, no," John said. "I'm flying home. Those bastards left us out here. Fuck 'em."

"You know I hate to fly," Meg said. "Let's just go to the Coast Guard station and let them take care of us."

John shrugged. Then he sat up straight and pointed.

"I see land," he said.

We all turned and looked.

"Right there, man. See it? It's right in front of us!"

I strained to see it, but I could see nothing but water.

"I think you're seeing things, bro," Brad said.

John slumped against the stern and sighed.

"So where would we fly, anyway?" Meg asked John.

"Probably to Portland. We'd go to my mom's."

"I don't want to fly there. I want to go to the Coast Guard station. I can't get on a plane like this. I might give someone this disease."

"What are you talking about?" I said to Meg.

"This thing I have. I don't want to give it to anyone."

"That's not a disease, Meg," I said. "It's blood poisoning. Nobody can catch it."

"I don't want to fly!" Meg said. Tears were spilling down her face. "John knows I can't fly. Please don't make me."

John put his arm around her.

"It's okay, Meg," I said. "You don't have to fly. When

we get there we'll put you on a train or rent a car or something . . ."

"Yeah, we'll do whatever you want," Brad said.

She continued to sob.

"Christ, Meg, shut up," Mark said and kicked at her. She wailed harder.

John didn't seem to notice. "We won't have to fly. We'll just get the car," he said. "We're right off Falmouth, so we'll just drive to the hospital where my mom works. She'll take care of us."

I couldn't believe John would tell Meg such a cruel lie. Then I realized that he believed what he was saying.

"We're not off Falmouth," Brad said. "We're out in the middle of the Atlantic Ocean somewhere. We're nowhere near Falmouth."

"Bullshit. It's right over there," John said with conviction.

"What the hell is wrong with you?" Mark said.

"Nothing's wrong with me," John said angrily.

Brad suggested Meg move up to the bow for a while. He thought if she tucked her legs up under the bow no one would be able to bump them.

"Deb and I can sit on the sides. And Mark can scoot to the back and you could stretch out a little more."

I nodded in agreement, though I wasn't happy about having to give up my spot.

"What about my foot?" Mark whined. "I need to stretch out, too. I want to get up there."

"Meg's in worse shape than you, Mark," I said.

"I'm going to sit up there next," Mark said.

John and Brad helped Meg slide up to the bow. John moved as if he were in a trance. His eyes were fixed and his movements slow and unnaturally deliberate. I sat up on the side for a few minutes, but I was too exposed to the wind, so I dropped down to the floor and leaned against the stern. Nobody said anything. I searched what I thought was the western horizon, looking for land, for anything.

"Quit it," I heard Meg say. "You're kicking me."

"I'm not kicking you," John replied.

"Cut it out."

"Quit bitching. All you do is bitch," John snapped.

"Where are my fucking cigarettes?" Mark suddenly shouted. His eyes were wide and wild-looking, and he was digging through the small mound of rotting seaweed in the bottom of the dinghy. "Who took them?"

"What are you talking about?" Brad said. "You don't have any cigarettes."

"What the fuck? You took them, didn't you?" Mark said to Brad.

"There aren't any cigarettes. Even if you did have some they would be sopping wet by now."

"I have cigarettes," Mark said slowly.

"Where'd you get them?" Brad asked.

"I just went to the Seven-Eleven and I bought beer and cigarettes. And I want to know who took them."

I stared at Mark in disbelief. He was out of his mind. Totally gone.

"Mark," I said, thinking I might be able to reason him

back to reality. "If you did just go to the Seven-Eleven, then why the hell did you come back?"

Mark sat in the rotten seaweed and stared down at his palms. He looked at Brad, then at me, then at Brad again. He blinked fast, as if he was trying to focus, then pulled his shoulders up toward his ears and winced and closed his eyes. He tried to speak, but the words seemed to get jammed up in his mouth.

"Wh-where a-are m-m-mmy bl-bl-oody cig-a-re-rettes?" he stammered and resumed pawing through the stinking weed.

Then Meg was shouting at John again and John was shouting back and Mark was ranting and I felt myself drowning in the sound of their voices, the whining, the shouting, the crying, the complaining. Why couldn't everyone just be quiet? I saw John kick Meg. He was doing it on purpose. She wailed and he kicked her again.

"Stop it, John," I said. "Don't you think she's in enough pain without you making it worse? Leave her alone."

John continued to jostle Meg. Meg continued to scream and cry. Mark was still trying to find his cigarettes. Finally Meg said she didn't want to be next to John anymore, so Brad and I helped her back to the stern. Mark immediately said it was his turn in the bow. While Brad and I were easing Meg back into position, I heard a strange noise. I turned in time to see John at the bow ripping off the rubber patch that secured the painter to the dinghy.

Brad and I hollered at John, but he pulled it off cleanly and threw it into the water before falling back against the stern. My knees buckled. I knew that in the next second the air would come hissing out of the Zodiac. I crawled forward, and Mark shouted, "Where the hell do you think you're going! It's my turn!"

I fell onto the bow and ran my hand over the rubber where the patch had been. Maybe I could plug the hole somehow, maybe there was a chance. To my relief, it seemed to be intact. There was no hole, no escaping air, no damage at all.

"Are you trying to kill us all?" I said to John, but I could see that he had no idea what he had done. His eyes were flat and dull. He was a million miles away. I knew he was in big trouble — maybe it was hypothermia or maybe the effects of drinking salt water.

Mark pushed me aside so he could claim his spot in the bow. I moved back to the spot where Mark had been sitting. Meg sat crumpled in the corner whimpering. I followed John's every move, terrified of what he might do next. I spotted the air valves in the stern. Please don't notice them, I said to myself. I willed John to look the other way.

I had to stretch. My legs were cramped and stiff. Mark had become engrossed again in searching for his phantom cigarettes, so I didn't think he would notice if I stretched my legs out straight just for a minute. As I unfolded them I saw how swollen they had become. The saltwater sores had grown, too. My skin looked as if someone had stubbed out big cigars on it. Some of the sores were red and hot and oozing. I wondered whether I would be able to walk once we got back to land.

Suddenly I felt a searing bolt of pain shoot up my left leg, through my groin, and up to the top of my head. I screamed and flew forward and slammed my fist into Mark's back.

"Bastard!" He had twisted my wounded toe. Blood spurted from it.

"Why can't you leave everyone alone?" Brad shouted.

"She's in my place," he said. "I want it back."

He pushed me out of the way and crawled to the port side. Brad and I moved back to the bow. I kept my eyes on Mark and John.

"Hey," Mark said to John. "Want a smoke?"

"Sure," John said. "Got any?"

"Under the seaweed. Up there." Mark moved toward the bow again.

"Mark. Listen to me, man. There aren't any smokes or beer or anything up here," Brad said. "We're out in the middle of the ocean."

"I got some sandwiches," John said. "You want one?"

It was pure horror, watching Mark and John carry on about their cigarettes and their sandwiches. They seemed to genuinely believe they had just been to the store and picked up supplies — as if they were just out on a day sail. They had both moved, simultaneously, into some other reality.

"Okay, where are they?" John hollered, picking up seaweed and tossing it overboard. "I know they were here."

"Where are my bloody fags?" Mark asked me. "I know you took them." He started to come at me, but Brad put up his hand to protect me.

"She doesn't have them, Mark," Brad shouted. "Leave her alone." Mark stared at us, then collapsed back against the side of the Zodiac. John slid down next to him, looking confused.

I slept. It was a tortured, fitful sleep, full of voices and cries. I awoke with the feeling that a shadow had just crossed my face. I sat up. Everyone was sleeping. It was dusk again. The clouds that had blocked the sun for so long were finally gone. I knew that this night was going to be colder than the others — the clouds, at least, had held in some warmth. Now I knew for sure where the west was, and I tried to convince myself that we were drifting in that direction. I watched the sky as we rode the swells and slid westward, toward land, toward life.

Meg's moans startled me. Had I been asleep again? The eastern sky was indigo-black now and pricked with a few bright stars. The western horizon still held some light.

"Meg," I said quietly. I didn't want to wake John and Mark.

She moaned again.

"Meg. Do you want to try sitting up here? You could stretch your legs out again."

"I want to sit up on the side," she said, and John's eyes opened.

"What?" John said with alarm.

"It's okay, John," I said. "Meg just needs to stretch out. She wants to get up on the side."

John immediately started to help Meg lift herself up. I was relieved to see him respond to her. Maybe he was okay. Whatever it was that had made him so irrational had been temporary.

Once Meg was up on the side, she said, "I've been thinking about it, and I've decided that if the Coast Guard wants to fly us to your mom's, it's okay with me. I just want to go home."

"We'll go straight home," John said.

"I don't normally like to fly, but —"

"I know, but just this once —"

"Yeah. I mean, it's probably the best way to go."

Brad woke up and listened to the two of them talk. Then Mark stirred. I felt myself go rigid with apprehension.

"See, that's west," Brad said. "We're definitely heading toward land. We have to wash up on shore eventually."

"When do you think?" Meg asked.

"Tomorrow, maybe the day after."

"I can't wait to see the look on the faces of those Coast Guard guys when we show up on their bloody doorstep," Mark said.

"Do you think they'll fly us in a private plane or a commercial plane?" Meg said.

"I can't believe they just left us out here," I said. "They never do that."

"What do you think, John, private or commercial plane?"

"Quit talking about planes," John said sharply. "I'm sick of hearing you talk about planes."

"I was just wondering —"

"We're not going on a plane. That would be stupid. I'm just going to go get the car."

"There isn't any car, John," I said.

"We're just off Falmouth. I know right where the car is. I'll go get it," he said. "You guys bring the boat in and I'll get the car. Then we can unload."

He sounded so sure, I had to fight to keep from being sucked into the fantasy. Was he right? Were we just off Falmouth? Then why . . . no, that wasn't right. It couldn't be. I closed my eyes and shook my head, trying to clear it, trying to stay focused on what was real. When I looked up again I saw John lowering himself over the side of the Zodiac.

"What are you doing?" Brad and I both hollered.

"I'll be back in a few," John said matter-of-factly.

"What about the sharks?" Mark asked.

"John, if you leave this dinghy we may not be able to get you back in," I said. "It's almost dark. Why don't you just come on back in now." I was trying to keep my voice even and calm. I had no idea what John was going to do, what might set him off. Was he just trying to get warm? Did he really think we were close to home?

"I can't take this anymore," he said. "I'm going to go get the car."

Brad and I looked at each other. John's hands slid away from the gunwale and he began to swim. He stopped for a minute, treading water and looking back at us. I thought he might be playing a sick joke. Meg was begging him to come back, pleading with one of us to go get him.

"Should I go after him?" Brad said to me.

I didn't know. I couldn't think. Was he really going to just swim away?

"Should I?" Brad sounded panicky. John turned and started stroking away from the Zodiac.

"John!" Meg cried.

"You can't go after him, Brad," I said. There was almost no light left in the sky. It would be impossible to force him back to the dinghy — and it could be suicidal to try. What if Brad went in and we lost him, too? We all watched John swim. Meg, her hands over her mouth, was shaking her head slowly and sobbing. John went up over a swell, disappeared, then reappeared farther off.

"Should I go?" Brad asked again.

"Don't go after him," Meg said quietly. "He's gone."

We rode up a big swell, and I saw John's head again, dark against the dark sea. And then we heard a terrible, gut-twisting scream.

"My God, he's calling me," Meg said and dissolved into tears.

We scanned the black water hoping for another glimpse of him. But Meg was right. John was gone.

9

Now we were four. I slumped against the rubber wall and buried my face in my knees and cried. I couldn't get that final scream out of my head. There was nothing else but that scream, no slapping water, no chattering teeth, nothing. I would never hear anything again but that scream. The only way to free myself of it was to go headfirst into the water, drown it, smother it, flood it out of my ringing skull.

I had to fight it. I started to say the Lord's Prayer again. Our father who . . . who . . . who . . . art in heaven

. . . Mark looked at me. I must have been saying it out loud. I didn't care. The words came haltingly, but they came, and the scream faded. As long as I kept saying these words I knew I was all right. It was my only proof that I had not gone mad, that I had not followed John over the edge.

Sometime during the night I asked Meg if she wanted to come sit with me. She looked at me with such confusion I had the feeling she didn't know who I was. She seemed to be in shock. I slipped under the bow cover and found Brad lying awake.

"Meg's in bad shape," I said.

"I know."

"If you want to sleep I'll watch you," I said.

Brad closed his eyes, and his face relaxed. I thought about his mother, how she must have watched him sleep a thousand times, just like this. She was probably the kind of mother who would smooth the blanket over you and touch your cheek and say things like "sleep tight."

I thought about the years I had lived in Fort Worth. My mother had just gotten divorced again and we had to move. I was miserable, starting another school in the middle of the year, a gangly seventh-grader trying to make kids like me even though I was new. I did my first hit of acid that year.

My mother traveled a lot, and when she was gone, I usually stayed with family friends I called Auntie Skeet and Uncle Jim. Though we were not related by blood, they treated me as their own. When I got into trouble, which was almost all the time, they disciplined me just as they disciplined their own daughter, Tisa, who was also my best friend. And I felt they loved me that way too. In my mind, I saw Auntie Skeet's open face and gentle eyes and heard her voice. She used to say things like "sleep tight."

The Zodiac made a sudden lurch. Somebody was moving around. Brad moaned and turned his head.

"Hey, lady," I heard Mark say. I held my breath. "I think it's about time you and me had sex." He was talking to Meg.

Brad opened his eyes. He had heard it, too.

"Oh, my God," I whispered. "We've got to do something."

"Wait. Let's just see how she handles it," Brad said.

We peered out, trying to see what was going on. Meg was still huddled in the corner. I saw Mark reach out and touch her face, then finger her matted hair. She began to cry. Mark pulled his hand away abruptly and said, "Fuck you. Fuck you. I'm tired of playing games. I'm going back to the Seven-Eleven to get some cigarettes."

Brad and I ducked out from underneath the bow. As we did, we saw Mark lowering himself over the side.

"Mark, stop!" Brad said.

"I'm not going anywhere," he said. "I'm just going to hang here a minute and stretch my legs." His voice had an eerie serenity to it.

I saw his pale hands moving, one over the other, along the side of the boat toward the bow. There was a metal handle on the front of the dinghy — I figured he was going forward so he could grab hold of it. Then I had a chilling thought.

"Brad, are there any patches up there? Do you think he's going to pull off the patches?"

We both scrambled forward to see what Mark was doing. I leaned over the port side but didn't see him. Brad looked over the starboard — no Mark. Now I was starting to panic. What was he going to do? Try to sink us? Flip us over? What twisted thing was he going to do next? If he went for the patches, I would kill him.

Brad startled me by plunging his hand down into the water. He brought it up with a small triggerfish wriggling in his fingers.

"I caught it!" he said. "There's a whole school of them. I caught it!"

I couldn't believe it — he had caught a fish with his bare hands.

"What do we do with it now?" he said.

"Clean it," I said. "Then eat it."

"With what?"

I remembered seeing my uncle gut a fish once by sticking his finger into the creature's belly and ripping it open.

"Give it to me," I said. As Brad handed me the fish, it slipped through my fingers and flopped into the bottom of the dinghy. We both scrambled to catch it again. Brad got it and held it out to me. I dug my finger into its soft white belly and dug its entrails out. Then I threw the guts, dripping blood, over the side and held the still-quivering fish out to Brad.

"Go ahead," Brad said.

I brought the fish up to my mouth and gnawed at it, but my jaws were so sore and my teeth so sensitive that I couldn't even break the skin. I handed the fish to Brad so he could try, but he couldn't break off anything either. The fish was just too tough and we were too weak. Brad threw the fish overboard in anger and I started to cry. To have food and not be able to eat it . . .

Suddenly something slammed into the Zodiac. In our excitement over the fish, we had forgotten about Mark.

"What's he doing?" I said as we were struck again. "Cut the shit, Mark!"

"Mark!"

We searched all around the edge of the dinghy, but we didn't see him. We felt for his hands. He was playing games with us. The dinghy spun again. He was going to kill us. He was trying to kill us all. In the darkness I could make out some turbulence in the water about ten feet off our port side. Then we were hit again, and I felt something under us, shimmying along the bottom. Another blow shoved us forward.

We were being attacked by sharks. I knew I was going to die. Time stopped. I heard Meg's frantic cries. I saw Brad's panicked eyes. I felt the rough skin scrape along the dinghy. The bow lifted up, then dropped back down. The dinghy spun around. I was paralyzed with terror.

Brad grabbed me and pulled me flat into the bottom of the dinghy. We clung to each other as the sharks continued their frenzied assault. We were being battered from all sides. They knew we were in here. They wanted us out. It was too much — the scraping skin, the blows, the frothing water, the screams. My mind bent around a corner, wanting to go down a road where there were no sharks, no seething water, no fear.

How would it feel to have the teeth clamp down on my legs? What if I didn't die immediately? What if I stayed alive long enough to feel another bite being taken out of my flesh, and another? What if the sharks tore Brad apart in front of me? Why not just jump in? Why not get it over with? Better to go quick than lie here like this, listening, waiting for the first hissing hole, for the hard rubber to go flaccid, for the platform to sink out from under us. I couldn't stand it another minute, the waiting, the absolute horror of it all.

I clutched Brad and felt such sorrow. It was over. No one would ever know how I died, how long I fought to hold on, how hard I tried, how much I wanted to live. No one would ever know that I had seen something in myself out here that I had never seen before. I had seen strength. I closed my eyes and prayed and waited to die.

Darkness. Water against rubber. Rising and falling. Something moving under the bottom of the boat. Sharks. Somehow I had fallen asleep even as the sharks hammered at us. And they were still here. I felt one make another pass, probing, trying to see if there was any more fresh meat, any reason to stick around.

Brad's eyes were open now, and he was listening, too, as the sharks continued to buffet the Zodiac.

"I have to sit up," he said suddenly. "I can't lie here anymore."

"They're still here," I said.

"I can't take it," Brad said. "Mark —"

"I know. They got him."

We were silent for a minute, then Brad said, "He was married, you know."

"You're kidding."

"They were separated. He felt really bad," Brad said.

Meg called out for John. Brad moved over next to her. I felt alone and abandoned at the bow, then I felt guilty for feeling that way. Meg needed Brad's body warmth more than I did. A shark made another slow pass along the dinghy. Waves of nausea passed through my trembling body.

"It's time to go," Meg said suddenly. "We're there." Her voice was light.

"Where?" Brad asked.

"We're there. Home. I'm going home."

"Not yet, Meg," I said. "We have to wait a while longer. Why don't you come up here and we'll all lie together and try to get warm until we get there."

She began crawling toward me without any assistance from Brad. She moved easily, almost gracefully. She didn't seem to notice the sharks butting up against the Zodiac. She simply lay down, stretched out straight, and sighed, as if she were relaxing on a warm beach. Brad and I lay on either side of her. I tried to hold my legs away from hers — I was so afraid that I would hurt her — but the motion of the boat forced me into her a few times. Oddly, she never cried out, never seemed to feel anything.

We lay like that for hours. Eventually I realized that the sharks had moved on. The water was quiet. I focused on the stars and tried to pick out a planet or a constellation. I thought that might give us a clue as to what direction we were drifting, and how fast. But I couldn't remember what to look for, how to connect the dots. Things I had known — where to find Venus, the shape of the Little Dipper — seemed to have been erased from my brain. Doors were shutting, one by one. Everything was going numb.

"I'm ready. Let's go now." Meg tried to sit up again, but Brad and I pulled her back down.

"Not yet, Meg," I said.

"Just a little while longer," Brad said.

I closed my eyes and instantly was awash in color and lights. Why did I see so much more when my eyes were shut? The black screen of my brain flashed staccato images, quick-cut fragments of people and places. It was as if someone was standing in front of me with a deck of cards and on every card was a scene from my life. The cards were flipping by fast, faster, until it was almost impossible to see what they showed.

There was my mother in a fancy pink dress, there was a herd of dusty cattle. There were rats in a grain bin, a tall peach tree, a grandfather clock beating time. There was the smell of saddle leather and sweat, of gin and vomit. A white car spinning on black ice, a tab of acid, bar graphs of cocaine on a cracked mirror.

There was a skinny kid who thought she was fat, a rich

kid who felt woefully deprived, a hungry kid who had made an enemy of food, a well-traveled kid who wanted nothing more than to stay home — no, to have a home. It was me, it was my life — my miraculous fucked-up life. I wanted more cards.

Brad was hollering. I had been asleep. I reached out for Meg. She wasn't there. I opened my eyes and saw her on top of Brad, clawing and snarling like a rabid dog. She flung seaweed in his face, and Brad shouted at her, then at me. When I reached out to Meg, she turned and went after me. I backed away, and she attacked Brad again. Screaming her name, I slapped her hard on the cheek, but she wouldn't stop. Brad shoved her, and she fell backward into the stern.

"Get away from me!" Brad shouted. His face was red and he was panting. "What's wrong with her?" I shook my head and watched Meg. She was making strange guttural noises, and her whole body was quivering.

"Do you think she drank salt water too?" I said.

"I was just trying to help her get warm." Brad was shaking.

"Leave her alone," I said. "That's probably the best." Brad and I lay down together again. Meg quieted down, and eventually I drifted off to sleep again. Sometime later I woke up and was instantly aware that something was different. The grogginess, the haze in my brain was gone. I saw everything clearly. I understood everything completely. There were the stars, the water, the two other bodies in the dinghy. There was the unforgiving enormous world. There was loneliness, fear, cold, the smell of Meg's festering wounds. The sky, I said to myself. Focus on the sky, on the beauty there.

I knew Meg was going to die soon. And, God forgive me, I felt relief. She was the last weak link. Once Meg was gone it would be Brad and me. We would be at square one, able to concentrate completely upon staying alive. And at that moment I knew with startling and absolute certainty that I was not going to die.

I crawled into the bow and lay down next to Brad. His eyes were open. I asked him if he thought the sharks were gone. He said he didn't know and closed his eyes. The putrid bottom water sloshed up around his face with every roll of the boat. I would stay here like this, watching him until he woke up, making sure he didn't drown in the swill.

✶

Meg was mumbling. I pulled myself out from under the bow to check on her. She didn't seem to hear me.

"Meg!" I said, louder this time. "Are you all right?"

She raised her hands and began fluttering her fingers, tracing lines in the air like a Spanish dancer. The movements were odd and graceful and unsettling. Then she spoke again in a low monotone, words that were foreign and incomprehensible to me but seemed to mean something to her. It was as though she was carrying on a conversation with someone in another world. I called to her again, but she didn't respond.

I reached back and grabbed Brad's hand and shook it.

Brad sat up, and together we watched Meg. She seemed calm, in control. The words flowed smoothly, like water in a summer stream. I had heard something like this before, but I couldn't think where.

"What's she saying?" Brad said, his eyes wide with amazement.

I shook my head. Where had I heard this? Where? Then I flashed to one hot summer in Texas. I was in a big airless tent filled with rows of folding chairs. Grandmother Queenie was there, and I was wearing a dress and singing "America the Beautiful" in front of everyone. There was a preacher. An old woman with heavy upper arms and smooth skin started to cry out in a language I had never heard. The people in the tent fell silent and turned to watch the woman. Some raised their hands to the sky. Others started to cry. I clutched my grandmother's hand in fear.

"What is she doing?" I asked her.

"Why, she's speaking in tongues, child," she said. "Praise the Lord."

*

"She's speaking in tongues," I said to Brad.

"What's it mean?" he said.

"I don't know."

Nothing we said or did brought Meg out of it. The words came, her hands danced against the night sky. She moved freely, apparently without pain. Was this

God speaking through her? Or was she talking to Him in a language known only to the dying? I was mesmerized and sickened by it.

Eventually Meg stopped chanting and lay flat in the bottom of the Zodiac. Her hands continued to flutter and her legs flopped back and forth, and then she started moaning again as if the pain was back.

"What can we do?" I said to Brad, choking back tears. "I think she's going to die."

"There's nothing we can do."

She moaned for a few minutes more and then was silent. Her eyes were open but glazed. Her body moved freely with the dirty water in the boat.

✔

I woke up with the sun on my face. Brad was sitting next to me staring at Meg. Her body had stiffened. Her skin was mottled with spidery blue blotches and riddled with deep sores, some of which had to be four inches across. The flesh around her deepest cuts, which had been so inflamed, had turned a pale green and become taut.

"She's dead?" I asked, knowing the answer. Brad said nothing. I bent over her face to see if she was still breathing. I picked up her wrist and searched for a pulse. There was nothing. I placed my mouth over hers and breathed out, trying to get life back into her.

"She's dead, Deb," Brad said. "She's been dead for hours."

"Oh, my God."

Damn you, I wanted to scream. Damn all of you for dying around me. Meg's body moved as the dinghy rocked.

"What are we going to do?" Brad looked at me. His eyes were wet.

"I don't know. I don't think we should keep her in the dinghy too long. Do you?"

"I don't think we could eat her even if we wanted to," Brad said. "She's too . . . I mean all the sores and everything . . ."

There was nothing to say. I was numb. I didn't even have the energy to cry. I sat back against the side and closed my eyes. I had to think for a minute. I became very aware of the sun on my skin, and I realized that my teeth had stopped chattering for the first time since we had sunk. I felt the Zodiac riding easily over the big rolling swell. I opened my eyes.

"I think we'll have to put her over the side," I said. "I don't like the idea but —"

"What else can we do?"

"We should take off her jewelry and stuff to give to her family."

"And her shirt. If we're out here much longer we might need it."

We sat there motionless a moment longer, then together we began to strip Meg's body. I took off her earrings, and Brad unclasped her gold chain. We both tried to remove the rings from her swollen fingers.

"I can't get it off," Brad said.

"Just do it," I said as I worked one off her left hand.

"I can't."

"Pull it," I snapped at him. I felt ill. I just wanted to get it over with.

I unbuttoned Meg's shirt, and Brad helped pull it off. There was no reason for her to be dead. She wasn't even supposed to be here. John had dragged her out here.

"Let's do it," Brad said.

"We should say a prayer or something. We can't just throw her."

"Say something."

I took a deep breath. "The Lord is my shepherd. I shall not want."

I stopped. Brad touched my hand. Then, louder, I continued. Brad and I said the Lord's Prayer together, and when we were done we picked up Meg's body and laid it on the side of the dinghy. We pushed her over and she floated away face down in the water.

"Don't watch," I said. "There might be sharks around."

We both lay down and closed our eyes. I was afraid of what I might hear. I felt as if I had just done something terrible, unforgivable. But what else could we have done?

When my aunt Ann died after her car was hit by a train, I remembered people in my family saying that death always comes in threes. Shortly after that another relative, Charles, was electrocuted, and then a friend of the family died of cancer. "Brad," I said, then stopped myself from going on. He'd think I was insane.

10

"Does anyone here know how to sail? Let's see hands."

"I do, I do." I wave my hand, lying.

"All right, Debbie," the counselor says. "Why don't you and Betsy take the first Sunfish at the end of the dock. Stay within sight of camp."

I push away from the dock and grab the tiller. The wind is hot and heavy with the musky green smell of lake water. The sail fills. We are flying. The camp dock is getting smaller and smaller. A towering thunderhead blocks the sun. I don't know how to turn the boat around. Betsy starts to cry.

We see two girls on the shore, and we both start hollering. The boat is picking up speed. I can't let go of the line. The girls turn and head back into the woods.

"They don't see us," Betsy is wailing. "We're going to die."

"Scream for help, Betsy. SCREAM!"

"Debbie, wake up." Brad was shaking me. "Debbie."

"I dreamed about my summer camp," I said. "The first time I ever went sailing. We got lost and there was a storm. Nobody knew where we went. Nobody could see us. It was awful."

"I've had dreams like that, too." Brad said quietly. He was so pale. Suddenly he leaned forward and retched, bringing up nothing. Then he collapsed backward against the side of the boat.

"Are you all right?" I said.

"I don't know. It's been going on for a while." He doubled over again and heaved. My God, Brad is dying. No. I won't let myself think that. Focus on something else, anything else. Brad and I are together. He will not die. We are going to stick together.

"We should wash out the dinghy," I said.

"I can't do that."

"Yes, you can."

"I just have to sit here awhile."

"You'll feel better if we clean it out. It's probably the smell of it making you sick. And with the sun out, it's only making it worse."

"No way."

"Doesn't it bother you that Meg lay here dead in this water and now we're sitting in it?"

"I don't want to wash it out right now. We just threw Meg overboard and I don't feel like getting in the water. Leave me alone. I don't feel good. I think I'm dying."

"Don't say that," I said. "You're not going to die. Come on, we're turning this thing over right now."

"The sharks."

"There hasn't been a shark around for hours. If they were going to come, don't you think they would have come for Meg? If you want, I'll stick my head in the water and look. Hold my legs."

"No."

"Hold my legs."

Brad moved toward me.

"If I start squirming, pull me in real quick, okay?"

I lay across the side and, with Brad gripping my legs, dunked my head underwater and opened my eyes. The salt stung, but in a few seconds my vision cleared. I looked under the dinghy and was startled by the sight of a big fish swimming toward me. But it wasn't a shark — it was opalescent and rounded, a silvery rainbow shimmering through the blue. Then I saw another one, and another. I recognized them — they were dorado, one of the best eating fish around. A school of them cruised under me. I had never seen anything so beautiful, so perfect, so full of grace. I squirmed so that Brad would know to pull me up.

"There's a school of dorado down there," I said to

Brad. "They're unbelievable. Like rainbows. You have to look. I'll hold your legs."

"I don't want to look," Brad said.

"But they're so fantastic —"

"If we're going to wash this thing out, let's get it over with."

I slid into the water. When I surfaced I saw Brad roll backward into the water off the starboard side. I gripped the polypropylene line, and Brad ducked under the dinghy and began to push it up. I pulled on the line, but the Zodiac didn't come toward me. This wasn't as easy as it had been a few days ago. I wondered if we had enough strength left to turn it over. Brad gave the dinghy one huge shove, and it landed upside down. I crawled under and splashed at the floorboards, trying to flush some of the filth away. The memory came to me of the five of us sandwiched under here the first night. How could they all be dead? I ducked underwater again and opened my eyes. I could see the dorado way off in the distance, and I felt bad that I had scared them off. I wanted them to be close to us again. It seemed very important to keep them close.

"Okay," I called to Brad when I surfaced. "We can turn her back over now."

Brad lifted his side of the Zodiac and I pulled from the other side, but no matter how many different angles we tried we couldn't get it to flop back over. Neither one of us had the strength to right it.

"This was your idea," Brad said angrily. "We may not ever get it over."

I began to cry.

"Don't," Brad said. "Just figure out how the hell we are going to get back in."

We tried again and again. Finally I pushed the leeward side toward Brad as he lifted the windward side, and the Zodiac flipped over and landed on my head. I reached up for the line and hung on with my cheek pressed against the hard rubber.

"Get in," Brad said.

I grabbed the line and Brad gave me a shove. I pulled and squirmed and groaned and eventually worked my way over the side and into the dinghy. Brad took the line and tried to pull himself in, but he couldn't get up high enough. I tried pulling him by the arms, but he was just too heavy for me — I couldn't budge him. We tried again and again. I started to panic. What if the sharks came back and Brad couldn't get in in time? What if Brad could never get back in? I pulled as hard as I could, and Brad slipped out of my grasp and landed back in the water. I fell against the side in tears.

"Debbie, stop. You have to help me."

My body shook with sobs. Why did I have to do everything? I couldn't do everything.

"Damn it, help me!" Brad screamed. I cried harder. I hated myself for making Brad get out of the dinghy. I hated Brad for not being able to get back in. We had to try again. I crawled across the dinghy. He got his hands up on the side, and I grabbed him by the belt loops of his blue jeans. I screamed and pulled with all my strength until somehow Brad came over the side and flopped onto the dinghy floor. He lay panting on the bottom of the boat, and I fell back against the stern.

"Shit," he said weakly. Then he rolled over and vomited. Seeing Brad this way devastated me. He had been my strength, my stability. I had linked my life with his life, tied my survival to his survival. If he died, where did that leave me? I was angry with myself for relying on him. His death would leave me weakened and more vulnerable.

"I'm not going to make it," Brad said.

"Don't say that. You are not allowed to say that."

We sat there in silence for a few minutes. The dinghy bobbed in the light chop. The sun played on the water. The world's blue beauty mocked us.

"Maybe we can catch a fish," Brad said.

"Of course we can," I said.

"And in a few days we'll wash up on a beach, and even if we are unconscious someone will find us and take us to the hospital."

He gagged and threw up again. Please, not Brad. His sister will never forgive me. Don't do it, God.

"You're okay, Brad. Your body just needs to do that, to get the bad stuff out. That's good. It's a good sign."

"You think?"

"I'm positive."

"You think if we catch some fish —"

"Definitely. There are fish everywhere now. They've come for us. We'll catch them and I know how to clean them and we'll eat them. Dorado — they're not so tough, you know? I caught them in St. Thomas. They're tender and sweet, and when we get one we'll divide it up and we'll live off that. And if we need to we'll catch some more and we'll just keep catching them until we wash ashore, until somebody finds us —"

"Debbie."

"— because I'm sure we're heading west and we're going to —"

"Debbie."

"— yeah, it sounds kind of far-fetched, but you don't know, you don't know, we might just see land in like the next minute or something —"

"Debbie. There's a ship."

The way he said it, so calmly, I thought he was hallucinating.

"There's a ship," he said again.

I turned around. There, indeed, off toward the hazy blue horizon, was a big ship. But I couldn't tell which direction it was moving. Like the others, I thought. It's too far away. It will go by.

"Don't waste your energy," I said. "It'll never see us."

But the ship got bigger, and bigger still. I couldn't believe it. It was coming closer, closer. I jumped up and began to holler and wave my arms so frantically that I lost my balance and fell into the bottom of the dinghy. I couldn't get back up. Brad and I lay in the bottom, powerless to do anything to attract the ship's attention, powerless to do anything but watch it go by.

The ship passed us. If someone had been on deck and if we had shouted, they would have been able to hear us — it was that close. But we didn't shout, we didn't do anything. It was a gray steel apparition, a barnacle-

covered mirage, a vessel of my desperate imagination —
what else could it be?

"It's going by," Brad said.

Then I knew it was real — it was real and close and it
was going to miss us. The ship moved on until at last we
were looking at its stern.

"At least we know we're still in the shipping lanes," I
said to Brad, fighting despair.

"Maybe we'll see another one today."

"Sooner or later," I said, "one of them is going to see
us."

I sat up again and watched the ship move away. Then,
slowly, ever so slowly, it seemed to be altering its course.

"Brad," I said. His eyes were closed.

"Mmmm?"

"Look."

Brad propped himself up. Was I wrong? Was the ship
still steaming away from us? No. It had turned. I could
see its portside flank. I could see the foreign writing
painted on its rusty hull. The ship was turning.

"I think it's coming back," I said.

I couldn't believe it. Had someone seen us? I was so
afraid to think that. But, dear God, the ship was coming
back. It did a wide U-turn until its bow was aiming
straight at us. It got closer, and I could see people scurry-
ing around on deck.

"Brad," I said, rising to my feet.

"I see them," he said. We both jumped and waved and
screamed as the ship passed our starboard side again. It
went by us, then made another excruciatingly slow turn.

It was off our starboard again, and this time I saw a man throwing a line out toward us. The line landed too far off. There was no way we could reach it.

"What do you think they want us to do?"

"It's hard to tell," Brad said.

"Do you think we should swim for it?"

"We can't reach it. They're going too fast."

"Wait till they make another pass. Maybe they can get closer."

The ship made another big circle around us and got within 150 feet of the Zodiac. A second line was thrown out, this one longer than the first and with a white life ring attached to it.

"I think they want us to try to swim for it," Brad said.

The ship made another pass. I could see the two life-lines cutting through the water no more than forty feet from the dinghy. This was our chance. I was going. I pulled myself up, went over the side, and began to swim. I stroked hard, finding a reservoir of strength somewhere deep in my soul. Forty feet felt like forty miles. The current was pulling me away from the line. I kicked harder. I could see the ring coming up fast, and I knew I had one chance to grab it.

The ring was there and I reached for it. I missed the hard foam but caught the rope. I closed my hand around it, around life. Then I lost my grip for an instant and felt the coarse rope burn my palm. Then I managed to get it in both hands, and now I was fighting to hold on as the swells tried to swallow me. I kicked my way to the surface, getting just enough time at the top to gulp air before I was hauled back down by the speed of the line. My hands slid again, and this time they were stopped by the ring at the end of the rope. I hugged the ring and rode, and prayed.

Where was Brad? I should have waited for him. Where were the sharks? I felt like bait on a hook. Why didn't I stay in the dinghy? Another wave forced me down. I was out of air, and water filled my nose and mouth. I'm drowning. Where the hell is Brad? Hang on, hang on. The line slackened a bit and I popped back to the surface. I searched the water for Brad, but the rope was jerked tight again and I was yanked under.

Something slammed into me. I kicked hard, my lungs screaming for air. Then I felt Brad next to me. He wrapped his arms around my waist and we both came up and gulped the air.

"I'm through the ring," Brad hollered. "Let go of the line. I've got you." I tried to open my fingers, but they were locked, fused to the hard rope. Brad was kicking hard, trying to keep us both above the surface. I forced my fingers to unclamp, and pain flashed up my arms. I reached for the ring and got it. Now I was facing Brad. There was a moment's slack, then the line snapped taut again and dragged us down.

My side scraped against something rough. When we surfaced again I saw that we were up against the hull. It rose, then came down on top of us. The force of the re-treating swell was sucking us under the ship. The barnacles tore at my skin. We were going to be crushed by the ship. Then, somehow, we were free of the hull and were being reeled in. The hull rose again, pinning us underwater momentarily. I tried to fend it off with my hands and feet, but the suction created by the ship moving through the water was too great.

We were against the hull, then we were away. We were under the ship, then we were free. We were underwater, then we were up in the air. And through it all, I could feel that we were slowly, slowly being reeled in. We surfaced, and I saw a gangplank being lowered and half a dozen men scrambling to get it into position. Just ten more feet, that was all we needed. The next swell raked us across the barnacles and forced us into the hull again. When we were sucked back out, I reached for the hands of one of the sailors as we passed the gangplank. I missed. We were washed back to the hull and pinned again. I waited to feel the surge of the retreating wave, but it didn't come. I needed air. I could feel the line being jerked, as if we were caught on something. I pushed and kicked and felt Brad doing the same. Air. I needed air, but I was drowning and I was too weak to fight it anymore.

A hand closed around my upper arm. Someone was pulling me up, dragging me up the hard metal grating of the gangplank. A wave crashed over me. I felt myself floating free. No! No! Then there were hands on me again and I was being carried. I looked for Brad. He was being carried up the gangplank, too. We were laid on the deck, panting and coughing and gasping as a circle of dumbfounded men with broad faces and ruddy skin closed in around us, speaking a language I didn't recognize. I didn't care what they were saying. I didn't care if they were from Mars. Brad and I were alive. We were safe.

The circle parted, and two fleshy middle-aged women with their hair in tight buns knelt down and began to undress me. They wrapped me in a blanket, then gestured to some of the men to pick me up. Brad and I were carried into another area of the ship — it seemed to be a sick bay — then placed in different rooms. I couldn't bear being separated from Brad. As soon as I was laid down on a gurney, I hollered for him. I could hear him calling my name. Several men came in and gathered around me. One of them had a stethoscope around his neck.

"Do you speak English?" I asked and got no response. Their language was thick and guttural and heavy. Greek, I thought. Or Turkish. No, they were too fair-skinned. The man I thought was a doctor left. I tried my high school Spanish and French on the others and got only blank stares and shrugs. When the doctor returned he was carrying a huge hypodermic needle filled with clear liquid. I watched as he held up the syringe and flicked it with his finger. My God, I thought, what is this guy going to do to me?

"Who are you?" I said again. "Where are you from?"

They all looked at each other and exchanged a few words. The doctor seemed to understand what I had asked. He said something to me and I caught a few syllables that sounded familiar. Something about their speech patterns, their growly consonants, reminded me of dialogue I had heard on television, in movies. These guys were Russian. We had been rescued by a Soviet ship! My first thought was that I was going to end up in the Soviet Union and no one would ever know what happened to me. And then I thought, who cares where I end up? I'm alive.

The doctor gave me the injection. Before he had withdrawn the needle I could feel my body relax. The two women returned and discussed something with the doctor. Then they came over, lifted me up, and carried me into a bathroom to a tub filled with medicinal-smelling water. As soon as my leg touched the water I screamed — they were trying to scald me to death. I kicked and squirmed and called for Brad as they tried again to lower me into the steaming tub. Finally they gave up and brought me back to the gurney.

Fatigue washed over me and I felt myself go limp. I lay back, detached and unresponsive, as the two women began to dab gently at my saltwater sores with a blue-green ointment. One of them slid a needle into my left arm and hooked me up to an IV. It all seemed so distant, so unreal, as if I were watching them work on someone else's body. I studied their faces; there was such kindness there, such sweetness. Tears filled my eyes. I wondered why we were so afraid of Russians. It was ironic. My country's worst enemy had been my salvation.

When they finished cleaning my wounds, one of the women touched my face and smiled. She closed her eyes, and I understood she was telling me to go to sleep now.

Sometime later I awoke, sweating and clawing at the needle in my arm. I had no idea where I was. This hard bed, these pea-green walls. Of course, it was a dream. In a second the curtain would lift and I would be back in the dinghy.

But those women peering at me and that steaming white metal cup — they seemed quite real. I took the cup and sipped. It was coffee laced with something potent — vodka, maybe. I couldn't drink it. One of the women left and returned with something that looked like ice cream, but that too was impossible to get down. Then a short man with a wide nose and dark hair came in, and the three of them talked among themselves for a minute and then turned to me.

The short man spoke.

"You . . . boat?"

"Yes, sailboat," I said. "From Maine."

"No more?" he said.

"Sunk in a storm. The windows broke. The boat was called *Trashman. Trashman.*" The three of them looked confused.

"Down," I said and made a sinking motion with my hand.

"Ah. Two peoples?"

"Five," I said, holding up my left hand and splaying my fingers apart. "Five people."

The man said something to the women, who shook their heads sadly. They all left the room, and I fell into a deep sleep.

I was awakened by the doctor and a younger, fair-haired sailor, who together were able to communicate to me that they had contacted the U.S. Coast Guard.

"Big surprise," the doctor said. "*Trashman.*"

"I'm sure," I said.

"Little bit problem. U.S. water. But okay now."

Slowly they made me understand that arrangements had been made for a rendezvous with a Coast Guard vessel. That news saddened me. I didn't want to trade my new Russian friends for the U.S. Coast Guard. I was too tired to go anywhere now. Why couldn't I just stay right here? The doctor gave me another injection and told me to sleep. I felt rivers of warmth flow through my body, then everything went dark.

✦

There was a flurry of activity around me. The two women were dressing me in some kind of green hospital pajamas. I looked at the doctor.

"Coast Guard," he said. I didn't want to move. Moving required energy and thought. I didn't want to do it; I didn't want to have to deal with the Coast Guard. There would be questions, lots of questions. And I had plenty of my own. I thought about Meg and John and Mark. It was so senseless. Three people dead in less than five days. If they had only hung on a little longer . . .

Some of the sailors came into the room and lifted me up. The doctor said, "You go now," and smiled.

When I got up on deck I could see the bright lights of a Coast Guard boat. Oh, how I had longed to see those lights five days ago. Brad was there, too. He had managed to walk out on his own. Overwhelmed with sadness, I began to cry. The Soviets eased me over to the four American sailors. I didn't want to go with them. I felt as if they — the Coast Guard — had abandoned me, left me to die.

"Wait," I screamed as they started to carry me away. I

needed another minute with my rescuers. I needed to say something to them. We kept moving toward the ship.

"I said wait!"

They stopped walking. I reached up and lifted the gold chain and cross off my neck. I wanted the Russians to have it. It was my only way to say thank you — I had to leave something of myself with them.

The doctor said no. But I took his hand and dropped the necklace into it.

"Ma'am, we really have to go now," one of the Coast Guardsmen said. "We've only been given so long to make this transfer."

I choked back tears as Brad and I were brought aboard the American ship. As I felt the Coast Guard boat pulling away from the Russian freighter, I broke down.

The boat ride seemed incredibly short. Suddenly we were at a dock, and the sailors were carrying me off the boat. Camera flashbulbs popped in my face and reporters shouted questions as Brad and I were taken up to two waiting ambulances. It was muggy and warm. There were haloes around the streetlights. I will always remember that, I thought as I was being slid into the back of the ambulance.

"What happened to the others? Are they dead?" I heard a woman yell. Then the doors slammed shut, and the high, mournful wail of the siren began to swoop through the night.

Epilogue

Brad and I spent eight days in Carteret General Hospital in Morehead City, North Carolina, being treated for exposure, acute dehydration, and massive infections. The day of our release we went out for lunch, along with my mother and Brad's mother and his brother Peter. It felt surreal sitting in the restaurant looking at a menu, watching the waitress try not to stare at the ugly crusted-over holes in my skin, and listening to my mother make small talk with the Cavanaghs. I wanted to scream.

Halfway through the meal Brad, who had lost a great

deal of weight, said he couldn't stand the pain of sitting on the hard wooden bench any longer. We all left and drove down to the waterfront in Beaufort. Brad and I walked out on the dock alone while our families hung back. We stood together and looked out at the placid, sparkling blue ocean. I started to cry.

That afternoon Brad left for Massachusetts with his family and I went to New Orleans with my mother. Being apart from Brad was strange and disorienting, but it was also a tremendous relief. I felt as if I had been detached from my Siamese twin.

𝄋

Of course I tried to sail again. What else was I going to do? I was a sailor — that was my job, my life. More than that, I wanted to believe I was strong, and I was certain that a strong person would get back on a boat as soon as possible. So, a little more than a month after our rescue, I took a job as cook and crew on *Shambala,* a Swan 65 that was a support vessel for *Nirvana,* one of the maxi boats racing in the Southern Ocean Racing Circuit, based in Fort Lauderdale.

Everybody seemed to know about *Trashman.* Some days I felt like wearing a sign around my neck that read "Yes, I am that Debbie Scaling." The sinking was big news in the sailing community, probably because it hit close to home for so many people. After all, we had been making a routine delivery, the forecast had been good, and as far as anyone could tell, we had been on a fine boat with a relatively experienced crew. I met with Morris

Newberger in Florida. He was sympathetic and wanted to help me — but I found it too painful to talk to him. I left his hotel in tears.

Other sailors told me how much they admired my toughness and resilience, but behind my back, I knew they were whispering about who had screwed up and how. People were always staring at me and pointing me out, so I took to wearing sunglasses almost all the time.

Things went fairly well at first. I got up in the morning, did my job, and didn't freak out. It wasn't until Brad unexpectedly showed up at my house in Fort Lauderdale that my control started to crumble. I hadn't seen him since we left the hospital. He had a British sailing magazine, and the cover photo showed Mark Adams with his pale eyes aglow.

"See, Debbie," Brad said, only half joking. "He *is* the devil. And he's haunting us."

I kicked Brad out and tried to ignore the hurt in his eyes. He didn't understand that it was torture for me to see him. I managed to get back on *Shambala* the next day, but I was a wreck. A feeling of "gloom and doom" took hold of me and wouldn't let go. Every minute that I was on the water I was terrified that something bad was going to happen, and when problems did come up, I was sure I would go berserk. Somehow I got through the next few months, but as soon as the SORC ended, I quit and went back to New Orleans.

Without the sailing, I was lost. Bulimia gripped me again. I drank heavily, got involved in a lousy relationship, fought with my mother, and was consumed with guilt for feeling so bad. You're pathetic, I would say to myself. You don't deserve to be alive. I couldn't make sense out of what had happened. Why had I lived? Why me?

I did my best to avoid everyone and everything that reminded me of *Trashman*, but at night all the memories would wash over me in a tidal wave of despair. In sleep's dark theater I relived it all — the tip of *Trashman*'s mast sinking away and John's ghastly final scream and the sharks' relentless assault on the dinghy. I saw Meg's lifeless body rising and falling and Mark's hands moving along the gunwale and the bloodied, frothy water. Most mornings I woke up to discover that I had wet the bed.

Despite everything, I found it almost impossible to stay away from boats. I still loved them — or at least loved what they had meant to me before the sinking — and I ached for the simple, innocent pleasure I had found in polishing brightwork, hosing down a gleaming deck, feeling a sail fill in a freshening breeze. It had been such uncomplicated joy.

In 1983 I enrolled in the Landing School of yacht design and boat building in Maine with the vague notion that I might be able to draw on my experience with *Trashman* to design a more stable boat. I bought a German shepherd, rented a cottage in Kennebunkport, and tried to dive into my studies. The people at the low-key farmhouse school were kind, but I wasn't able to cope with kindness. I was floundering, and the news that Morris Newberger had built another boat, painted it green, and christened it *Trashman* sent me into a tailspin.

Before the first semester was over I was drinking again, sleeping late, missing classes, and ignoring assignments. I ate and ate and ate, trying to fill that bottomless hole in my gut. And I spent hours alone in the small Catholic church praying for someone or something to help me.

The only good thing that happened to me that winter was running into John Kiley at the boat show in New York City. I had met him the summer before in Newport during the America's Cup. John had sailed around the world in the early seventies on a thirty-foot Tahiti ketch. We had lunch in New York, then saw each other again two weeks later. I found that he was the first person who really understood when I talked about *Trashman*. I felt a surge of hope. I was going to get my life in order, fight the bulimia, throw myself into schoolwork, get back into sailing.

But then someone ran over my dog, John went to the Caribbean with his old girlfriend, and I went surfing with Woody. And then I ran.

I spent spring break in Texas with my father and stepmother, trying to pull myself together. Thanks to them, and to friends like Auntie Skeet, Uncle Jim, Tisa, and Dave, I slowly began to get stronger. I started to see that part of my difficulty in dealing with the sinking was that I had so many unanswered questions, particularly concerning the Coast Guard.

I was very troubled by inconsistencies I had heard about in their search and rescue reports. Among the most baffling was their claim that they had received a call —

just hours after the boat sank — from an unidentified person saying that *Trashman* was safely moored in Wilmington, North Carolina.

I wanted to know what they thought had happened to us — and why they had apparently canceled the search without first trying to confirm reports that we were safe. When Tisa took me out to look for a lawyer who could help me, we were advised to find someone back east. Eventually I found a top marine law firm in Maine; the attorneys there convinced me to file a lawsuit against the U.S. Coast Guard.

After I returned to the yacht design school in the spring of 1984, John Kiley came back into my life with the news that he had broken up with his girlfriend. John was working for a yacht design firm in Boston, and I began commuting to see him on weekends. After several months we became engaged. John made me feel safe and sane and, for the first time in my life, truly loved. And he was a tireless listener who never once judged me. I got control over the bulimia and felt that my life was finally turning around.

John and I were married in the fall of 1984 and had our first child nine months later. The night before I gave birth to Marka, I had a devastating dream in which I was treading water and holding my baby over my head while we were being circled by sharks.

A little more than a year later, our second child, John IV, was born. Just before his birth, I agreed to settle the lawsuit with the Coast Guard. After two excruciating years of depositions and interrogations, my lawyers advised me to put an end to it, even though none of my questions had been answered satisfactorily. I didn't have the strength to fight anymore. I had a family to raise.

But through all the happy confusion of having two small children in the house, there was never a day that I didn't think about *Trashman*. Sometimes the memories overwhelmed me. One minute I would be standing in the shower washing my hair, and the next minute sitting in the tub sobbing uncontrollably. And I was never free of the dreams.

It was particularly hard to see Brad. He continued to sail, with an intensity that I attributed to a burning need to prove himself over and over again. He often stopped at our house outside of Boston to crash for a day or two before going off again. He and John became friends, and the three of us spent many long nights talking about Mark and Meg and John and what had gone wrong on *Trashman*. Brad's visits always left me shaken.

I marveled at his ability to get back on the water. I found I couldn't even look at the ocean without reeling. Although I had married a yacht designer with several boats and a summer house on Cape Cod, I could hardly bring myself to put my feet in the ocean, never mind get on a boat. John never pushed me, but I always felt that I was letting him down. I forced myself to do a few brief harbor cruises with him, but I was miserable the whole time. I couldn't stand the feel of the wind on my face.

John and I went through difficult times, and in 1987 I left him briefly and took the children to Texas. I was terrified that my bulimia was going to start up again. I went to church and started seeing a counselor twice a week. She helped me see that I was still running and that until I was willing to do the hard work of dealing with what I was running from, I would never be happy. Eventually I found help with Overeaters Anonymous and Adult Children of Alcoholics. I went back to John five months later, determined to make our marriage work.

There were many obstacles to overcome, but I slowly learned how to handle the destructive issues in my life. Little by little, I was getting back on decent terms with my mother. But I still needed a way to deal with the sinking of *Trashman*. In 1990 I decided to try to put it all down on paper.

*

Writing *Albatross* has been stressful. On many days I wanted to give up, feeling I just didn't have the strength to replay it all in my mind. I sought aid from therapists and hypnotists and psychiatrists until I found one who helped me understand that I was suffering from classic post-traumatic stress disorder. I wasn't crazy, I just needed a way to exorcise the demons of the past before I could move on, once and for all.

Writing this book has helped me to do that. And, miraculously, it has also given me the strength to sail again. In the summer of 1992 I decided to do a three-weekend, six-race series on *Venture,* John's Wianno Senior, a twenty-five-foot gaff-rigged wooden boat.

The first four races went fairly well even though we

had a minor collision with one of the other boats in the fleet. We were way back in the standings, but I felt great. I was holding it together, I was sailing.

The morning of the fifth race dawned clear and hot and windy. By the time John and I boarded the Hyannisport Yacht Club launch, the wind had picked up considerably. The club was celebrating its seventy-fifth anniversary, and the fleet was huge, with everything from 5-0-5's to Lasers to Beetle Cats. I noticed a small boat being towed in, then another and another. One Cape Cod Knockabout had been completely swamped. My stomach began to churn, and my shoulders got very tight. I heard someone in the launch say that some of the races had been canceled because so many of the smaller boats had capsized.

I felt the old gloom and doom threatening to close in, but I fought it off, reminding myself that Seniors needed a lot of wind just to get going. The wind was a gusty 30 knots from the north-northwest and building, and it was a wet beam reach to the mouth of the harbor. Once we got outside the breakwater, the full force of the wind hit. All around us smaller boats were being knocked down.

John and our crew, Peter and Stewy, were busy getting ready for the start. I was busy having a conversation with myself. We're not going to stay out here, are we? It's okay, you're with John, I told myself. Am I losing my mind? You're doing fine. No, I want to get off. You're okay. I have to get off. You'll be okay. I'll die.

"Okay, guys, pay attention out here," John said. "Let's harden up."

With that we cranked in the sails until we were hard on the wind. Peter and I crawled out on the windward rail, almost immediately taking a huge wave over the bow. The water hit me in the face, burning my eyes and filling my mouth. Don't panic, don't panic, I chanted to myself, but it was a losing battle. I was dizzy and my chest was heaving.

"Let's ease everything out and go check out the starting line," John said. I couldn't believe how calm his voice sounded, how controlled. Focus on John, I told myself, and do the job.

We maneuvered through the fleet as it converged near the start. The ten-minute gun went off, then another one sounded, signaling a postponement. My heart lifted. The winds were too high — they'd have to cancel! We sailed around while we waited for the judges to make their decision. At some point we noticed a small tear in the mainsail, but in these conditions it was impossible to fix it on board. We'd definitely have to go in now, wouldn't we? To avoid a larger tear?

"They dropped the postponement flag," John said. We were going to race. Everyone cheered but me.

The start gun sounded, and the weighty ballet of creaking wooden hulls and flapping canvas began. We squeezed over the starting line on a starboard tack, waiting for the fleet to spread out before coming about. The wind was coming in huge erratic gusts, and I was on the weather rail eating waves.

When we finally saw the mark, we bore off and began to get the pole and spinnaker ready for the next leg. As one of the lead boats rounded the mark, I saw a huge wave sweep across its deck and wash the spinnaker right out of its bucket. Filling with wind, the billowing sail began to pull the boat over on its side. Somehow, at the last minute, the crew managed to regain control.

"I don't know if we can carry a chute in this, John," I said, hoping he wouldn't make us try.

"We'll see," he said. The two boats in the lead hoisted their spinnakers.

Shit, I said to myself.

We rounded the mark in a big group, then came down a bit, hoisted our chute, and took off.

"We're in fourth place," Pete said.

A big gust knocked us over on our side, but Stewy managed to let the mainsheet off in time to right us. I was quivering with adrenaline, beyond fear, beyond rational thought. My only goal was to keep from going completely insane as the wind pummeled us and the shimmying boat surfed the waves.

I may have screamed when I felt the huge gust hit us. I know I turned toward John, searched his face for reassurance, and, to my horror, found none. I saw the starboard running backstay let go and then saw the thick wooden mast snap like a dowel, taking everything — lines, blocks, wire rigging, canvas — over the side with it. John's face registered his astonishment as he turned to look at me.

Then something even more astonishing happened. I didn't cry or crumple to the deck. I didn't come undone. Something bad, very bad, has just happened, I said to myself, and I'm still breathing. I'm all right.

"Okay, guys," I shouted, startled by the power in my voice. "Let's get this rig in next to the boat before it does any more damage. Somebody get a screwdriver so we can get this mainsail off. Let's get these sails out of the water." I saw John smiling at me, and I knew that he knew.

We got towed back to our mooring and took the launch ashore. Everyone at the club rushed out to see if I was okay. I think they expected that I would have to be carried off the boat.

"Let's get another mast," I said to John on the way home. "Let's race tomorrow."

So that's what we did. We worked well into the night to get *Venture* rerigged; we were still working on her as we were being towed out to the starting line. But when the gun went off at 2 P.M., we were ready, much to the amazement of the rest of the fleet. We got a great start and stayed near the front as we rounded the first mark. We were in fourth place, then third, then second. I looked back and smiled at John and gave him the thumbs-up sign.

I felt the sun on my face and tasted the salty spray and heard the sweet high hum of the rigging. I shook my fist in the air and shouted. John found more wind, and I felt the boat lifting, skimming the small waves, shuddering with speed. It was as if she were trying to take off. Water splashed up and over me, and I shouted again at the pure, clean joy of it all. And at that moment I knew, knew with all my heart, that these weren't just sails I was under. They were wings.

Appendixes

.

Coast Guard Report on the Sinking of *Trashman*

Excerpts from the final report of the investigating officer,
United States Coast Guard Marine Safety Office,
Wilmington, North Carolina.

At 0654, 24 October, TRASHMAN made radio contact with USCG Station, Georgetown, SC. This contact was stated by TRASHMAN to be a position report, not a mayday, and that they were hove to without power. . . . At 0710, TRASHMAN made radio contact with USCG Group, Charleston, SC. At that time he reported his position. . . . TRASHMAN advised Charleston that they were under sail making 5 to 5½ knots, that the propulsion engine was not working and the batteries were getting low. They also stated they were not in any danger at that time. Charleston advised TRASHMAN that Wilmington, NC was the closest port, and TRASHMAN agreed to make for that port even though doing so meant going broadside to the wind and sea. . . .

At 0855, John Lippoth told Group Charleston, "I think I'm going to have to ask you for Coast Guard assistance." . . . He reported his position. . . .

At approximately 0925, Mark Adams reported to Charleston that they were no longer taking on water and were "just experiencing a little heavy air," but still requested Coast Guard assistance. Fifth Coast Guard District RCC ordered a C-130 aircraft from Elizabeth City, NC to locate the vessel and render assistance. . . .

At 0950, CG 1347 (C-130 aircraft) was over the TRASHMAN. They observed . . . an extreme amount of spray in the air at sea level, and the TRASHMAN lying broadside to the waves. . . . Radio contact was established between the aircraft and TRASHMAN during which it was determined that no immediate assistance was needed except a tow which the aircraft was not capable of. At 1105, the aircraft advised the TRASHMAN to secure their electronics to conserve battery power and to energize their radio for an hourly communications check. They also advised TRASHMAN that the M/V GYPSUM KING (UK) was enroute with an estimated time of arrival of five and a half hours. The GYPSUM KING had been asked for assistance by Fifth Coast Guard District RCC at 1020 and immediately turned into the seas and weather to make for the TRASHMAN. The aircraft did not advise Charleston of their observations or their advice to the TRASHMAN. The aircraft then departed to search for the S/V OBLIGATION. The aircraft experienced a generator failure in one engine and a severe windshear on the way to the OBLIGATION, and the aircraft commander decided to go to Wilmington, NC, rather than risk the lives of the crew.

At 1200, TRASHMAN made a communications check with Charleston, and reported their position. . . . Charleston informed them that the ETA of the GYPSUM KING was 2000. Charleston did not have any communication with the GYPSUM KING. Charleston then requested TRASHMAN to secure all power and contact them at 1300. . . .

At 1313, Charleston attempted communication with TRASHMAN without result but did not initiate a search. After this, no effort was made by any Coast Guard unit to contact or search for the vessel. . . .

From 1550, 24 October to 0000, 25 October, the EXXON HUNTINGTON hove to because of the weather approximately 6½ miles WSW of the TRASHMAN's reported noon position.

At approximately 1535, Coast Guard Group Charleston received a call from an unknown person stating that the TRASHMAN was under way for Wilmington, NC.

At approximately 2110, Coast Guard Group Charleston received a message from an unknown person that the TRASHMAN was safe in Wilmington, NC. . . .

On 28 October, . . . a Russian fishing vessel, the

OLENEGORSK, VHBS discovered the raft with the two survivors.... The survivors were brought to shore at Morehead City, NC.

On 2 November, the [Zodiac] raft was found by the S/V BELLE VAN ZUYLEN near Diamond Head Light, Cape Hatteras, NC. The raft was taken to Ft Lauderdale and identified by Deborah Scaling as belonging to the TRASHMAN....

APPENDIX B
Rescue by the Russians

The following newspaper article, translated from Russian,
was written by Dr. Leonid Vasiliev, ship's doctor
on the freighter Olenegorsk.

On October 28, 1982, the freighter "Olenegorsk" was carrying a load from Cuba to Canada. Weather conditions were poor: winds of 7–8 knots, waves of 3–4 meters. Around twelve noon, 170 miles off the American coast (off the state of North Carolina) the navigator on duty, Yu. P. Kaveshnikov, sighted at great distance a small boat carrying people, who were signaling urgently for help.

About a week earlier, a hurricane had struck the East

Coast of America, and several vessels had been sunk. News of the disasters was received by radio from the Coast Guard.

Our ship changed course as soon as we saw the survivors, and went to their rescue. Coming nearer, we saw a small inflatable boat in which a boy and girl were sitting. From a distance of 60–70 meters they seemed to us to be perfectly happy. Their clothes and smiling faces did not in the least reflect the tragedy they had experienced, and about which we then knew nothing.

A decision was made to swing about, to approach closer to the boat, throw out a line, draw in the boat and bring the young people aboard. As a result of the high seas and strong current, our first attempt was not successful. Only after coming about three times did we manage to get within 40 meters of the boat.

Our experienced boatswain, A. M. Zaichenko, gave the order to throw astern a life buoy on a long line (more than 100 m. in length) and to throw out two other short lines to port. As it turned out, these precautions were not taken in vain.

Sailor A. Antonov threw out the line, but as if to spite our plans, it fell short of the boat by a few meters. The current was carrying the survivors farther from us all the while. Misunderstanding our intentions, first the boy and then the girl abandoned the boat and jumped into the sea, trying to swim to the line.

The boy reached it and grabbed the ring with both hands, but the girl was washed away by a wave and carried along the ship's side by the current. When he saw this, the boy let go of the ring and swam after the girl. The people standing on deck watched with horror as the two were swept away by the current; time and again they were covered by high waves. Tragedy seemed imminent.

Thanks to the line attached to the life buoy, which had been thrown out over such a long distance, we nevertheless managed to pull the couple from the water. The boy and girl clung obstinately to their last hope — the life buoy. Unfortunately the ship had not come to a full stop, and this fact, together with the play of the line, which sometimes snapped taut, made it seem that the rope might break apart. Forming a chain along the side of the ship, six crew members slowly began to haul in the buoy, and with it the survivors. From time to time the human figures disappeared beneath the waves, and we thought nothing but the buoy was left. This time, though, fortune was on our side. We managed at last to pull the couple to the gangplank, which had been let down just in time.

Wearing a life jacket and secured by a line, carpenter Yu. Dogarev lowered himself down the steps and was able, with great difficulty, to pull the two survivors in the nick of time onto the main gangplank. Just then, a sudden wave engulfed all three of them. The evil ocean made a last attempt to tear from us those who had been fated to perish. But our Yura was master of the situation and held the survivors on the gangplank.

The boy and girl had absolutely no strength left; they couldn't move without assistance and were quickly taken to the ship's sick bay. Both showed symptoms of shock, hypothermia, and dehydration, their skins were covered with many running sores. Intensive care was administered, blood transfusions, warming, etc.

When their condition had improved, the two survivors told us about themselves and the unhappy events they had experienced.

Debby Skanding [sic], 21, was from New Orleans, an experienced yachtsman who had navigated the waters of many different countries.

Brad Cavanaugh, 22, was from Massachusetts, a university student.

On October 22 they and some friends had left Florida for the Bahamas on a two-masted, 50-foot yacht. The five-man crew included two women and three men. The day after they set sail, a severe storm blew up, during which one of the boat's masts was broken. Shortly thereafter, a porthole was smashed open by a wave; the yacht began to fill with water and sank in a matter of minutes. This took place on the morning of October 23. All five of the crew managed to get into a small, inflatable life raft. One of the girls, evidently overcome by such stress, soon died, and it was necessary to give up her body to the stormy sea. A school of sharks circled the raft, according to Brad and Debby, heightening the level of tension. The situation was made worse by the fact that the life raft did not live up to its name at all; it contained no blankets, no food and none of the equipment which a life raft should have on board for emergencies.

Five days and five nights the raft drifted on the open sea. The extreme nervous tension, fear, hunger, and thirst took their grim toll. Two of the men lost their minds. One of them said he was going to a bar for a beer and a cigarette, and jumped into the sea. The second followed suit a little later, only a few hours before the moment when the survivors were sighted by the navigator on duty on our ship.

Debby and Brad emphasized that in the course of the five days and nights, several ships sailed past them, including one American ship, but that no one came to their rescue.

As a sign of their gratitude, the Americans kissed our hands, and Debby tried to show her thanks by giving us the chain hanging around her neck.

The entire crew showed great concern and attention for the survivors; almost everyone tried to ease their condition in some way, and all were very worried about their health. And it called for concern. As a result of hypothermia and exhaustion, both began to suffer from an inflammation of the lungs.

The ship's radio officer made contact with the U.S. Coast Guard; it was decided to take the survivors to the nearest American port, where they would be transferred to hospital. Debby and Brad were on board with us for about twelve hours; near midnight on October 28, our ship anchored off the port of Beaufort. We dressed the rescued Americans in warm woolen clothes and carefully carried them on board a small Coast Guard cutter. Brad and Debby expressed their extreme gratitude to us for their rescue and apologized that they could not at that time add any material token of their thanks. They did not know that such an idea is foreign to Soviet sailors. Our greatest rewards were the elevated spirits, the feeling of satisfaction at the saving of human lives.

On the following day, J. Costello, the commander of the Fifth Section of the U.S. Coast Guard, sent a telegram to our captain, expressing gratitude to the entire crew for our action in rescuing the two survivors, action taken, in his words, in the best of maritime traditions.

A week later our ship reached Montreal. We telephoned New Orleans, hoping to find out from Debby's parents what state of health she was in. To our surprise and joy, Debby herself came to the phone and told us she felt fine and was under medical supervision, and that Brad was also in good condition. The last words which the American girl pronounced were, "I love all Russians."